Who is, This,
JESUS ?

CLIFFORD AUTEN

WESTBOW
PRESS®
A DIVISION OF THOMAS NELSON
& ZONDERVAN

WestBow Press books may be ordered through booksellers or by contacting:

WestBow Press
A Division of Thomas Nelson & Zondervan
1663 Liberty Drive
Bloomington, IN 47403
www.westbowpress.com
844-714-3454

ISBN: 978-1-6642-8029-8 (sc)
ISBN: 978-1-6642-8030-4 (hc)
ISBN: 978-1-6642-8031-1 (e)

Library of Congress Control Number: 2022918676

Print information available on the last page.

WestBow Press rev. date: 10/09/2023

Preliminary

Written by a non-scholar

The writer is not presenting himself as a bible scholar, nor does he present himself to be anything other than what he is --- a Christian who has been observant, generally without a judgmental eye, but wondering why we do what we do and how can we do better to exemplify Christ in our lives; and, why should we?

The main body of the book is a prose designed to present Jesus from the beginning through the end of time as described in the Bible. From the perspective of one whose chosen behavior resulted in the need of the Savior, the writer presents the true perspective of being personally responsible and personally participating in as well as observing the barbaric crucifixion process Jesus suffered to provide Himself as the chosen Lamb of God.

Each verse of the prose is supported by scripture and each scripture is presented to the reader using five translations for the reader's convenience for comparisons. The writer's hope is for the reader to study the scriptures, compare them from different translations, view them in context of the surrounding verses, and more clearly see how Jesus is presented to us in the Bible.

"Who is, This, Jesus" began several years ago as a song to praise the Lord for who He is and what He has chosen to do for mankind. With time, more verses were added until they would not fit in as a song so it changed to a poem, and then more were added until the rhyming was not consistent thus the author has chosen to consider it a prose. Please read it as though someone is speaking it rather than as an English composition. Some punctuations, capitalizations, etc., are for emphasis and hopefully will not confuse you. The first presentation is without footnotes intentionally for fluidity of reading. The second presents footnotes to validate each phrase or sentence as being supported by scripture. Then are the scriptures coordinated with the footnotes to simplify the access of scripture for the reader.

Following the prose, the writer gives his personal opinion as a non-scholar as to how to apply Biblical truth into daily life and why we should pursue doing so; followed by two poems written by the author for the enjoyment and hopefully encouragement of the reader.

Translations used:

NASB --- New American Standard Bible 1995
AMP ---- Amplified Bible
CJB .... Complete Jewish Bible
KJV .... King James Version
NIV .... New International Version

Pre-introduction

We were not present when Christ was born, yet we believe. We were not present when He was crucified or raised from the dead, yet we believe. For there was a time for each of us who believe when we were drawn by the Father to accept His Son Jesus Christ as our Savior. He, through the Holy Spirit entered our hearts, joined to our spirits, and we were born again. We who believe have been saved by His grace and cleansed by His blood through faith (trust). Adopted as sons and daughters of the Most-High God, being beneficiaries of the most cruel, barbaric, and brutal process of our Lord's crucifixion; how shall we escape the chastisement of our Heavenly Father if we view carelessly and neglectfully so great and so costly salvation which we have freely already received? And, how shall we serve Him appropriately unless we know who actually is this One to whom we profess to serve?

Introduction

Generally speaking, when I read a book, I do not like to read the introduction. Personally, I am a very slow reader and am not patient enough to use the time. My primary interest is to get into the "meat" of the book pertaining to why I bought the book in the first place. If you are of the same mind-set, I ask you to make an exception here.

To perhaps better grasp what is shared in the following, come with me in your thoughts and imagine yourself walking on a sidewalk in a busy town. You are not alone. There are many people walking with you and you are all walking in the same direction. To your right are businesses and to your left is a busy one-way four lane street with a lot of traffic going the same direction as you. Beyond the street is another sidewalk and businesses, but everyone there is walking opposite to you and the cars. As you walk along, you look across the street and suddenly, there it is! There, right across the street from you is what you have heard about for years but had never found. It is the best ice cream parlor in the world! They have anything you can possibly want and their servings are huge! Their toppings seem unlimited and they have a half-price sale sign out! On top of all that, you are hungry and you have money!!

It's all right there before you, right across the street. You look ahead of you to see the traffic light and crossing. It's way, way down there and the sidewalk is too crowded to run. What you want is right across the street. Facing the street, you look to your left at the busy traffic in all four lanes. Frustration sets in. You don't want to wait. Your goal is right there across that four-lane street. Suddenly, you notice a break in the traffic approaching you. Yes! The break isn't very long, but you are hungry and you are fast. You used to run the hundred-meter dash in school and that road isn't nearly that wide. As soon as this next car goes by you can make it. There's no other break in sight and the traffic is going at least 30mph but if this next car will just hurry up and get out of your way you can make it across. Now! Go! Quickly! Quickly! You're sprinting like a pro! One lane crossed, two lanes behind you. Then, you notice something in front of you before the fourth lane. It's just some water from the light rain earlier today. Not much but you cannot jump over it, you'll just run through it. No problem! Your left foot hits the shallow puddle and suddenly it slides out to your left. The water is mixed with oil residue from the road and is slick as ice, but it didn't look that way. None-the-less your left foot traction is gone, gravity grabs you, and in an instant, you are down! Stunned by the shock and confused at what happened you get to your knees and try to stand but your foot slides again. You're back on your knees. Then, suddenly, you realize where you are and you think "the traffic!!". Instantly, you hear the blast of a horn, the screaming of people, and the screeching of tires from the locked brakes of the truck you see approaching you. In a fraction of a second you see smoke coming from the tires of the eighteen-wheeler, cars to the driver's right and the crowded sidewalk to his left. There is no place for him to go to avoid you. You realize, you are on your knees and you are about to die.

Something has happened. You feel the pressure on your arms of large, strong hands grasping you and suddenly you are in the air being thrown to the sidewalk you were approaching. You hit the concrete and roll to safety. There is still a lot of noise -- people yelling, horns blaring, tires screeching as they pass by you. Then, silence. Not a sound, followed by people yelling, "Hurry! Where is he!? There! There! He's under the truck!" You don't remember getting up but you find yourself pressing through the crowd to see what has happened. You watch as some men pull at someone from beneath the truck. He was caught and dragged three or four times the length of the eighteen-wheeler before the driver could stop. Nothing appeared to be broken, but his clothing was ripped from his body. He had been struck hard by the truck then dragged beneath it. He was bearded but much of it was torn from his face. His shoes were torn off and his hands and feet looked as if someone had beaten them with spikes. His back was strangely torn, as though scourged with a whip.

Why did he do that? Why did he grab you and throw you to safety knowing he would be taking your place of certain death? You think to yourself, "I didn't ask him for help. It's not my fault. He didn't have to take my place." Then you realize in honesty, "If I had only followed the law. Jay-walking is such a minor offense but my choice to break that law was going to cost me my life; and he took my place. It was my fault. But he didn't have to do that. I don't know him, yet he took my place. That torn and bleeding man took my place by his choice." It was clear. "He chose to take my place."

That evening you saw the news cast about the man. He lived for about six hours from the incident. He had no broken bones yet he lost a lot of blood. For some reason he refused pain medication. Through those six long hours his pain was terrible and his breathing labored. It was more than his body could stand. Finally, he died. He took your place. He loved you and you didn't even know him. You could have obeyed the law and gone to the traffic light and cross-walk. Then he would not have had to choose between your life or his own. But you didn't do that, and he chose to take your consequences. He chose to take your place.

Jesus chose to take our place. We, by choice, have chosen sometime in our lives to violate God's Law. As minor as it may have seemed to us, that chosen action cost us our relationship with God our Creator, yet, before we knew Him, He took our place. So, who is He? My hope is the following will help you better understand.

Prose

Who Is, This Jesus

The book of "Acts of the Apostles" – chapter 2 – the day of Pentecost. Thousands came to the Lord that day. Peter, addressing the multitude: "This Jesus whom you crucified-- by the hands of wicked men…." This was weeks after the crucifixion. Surely, most of those people were not there. As, neither were we. "This Jesus, whom YOU crucified by the hands of wicked men…" Nor were they before Pilot crying "Crucify Him! Crucify Him! Give us Barabbas! Crucify Jesus!" Again, neither were we. So, as is written in the Bible--- who is this Jesus whom WE crucified--- by the hands of wicked men!?

In the beginning, was the Word. And the Word was with God, and the Word was God. All things were made through Him, and without Him nothing was made that was made [Jn1:1 NASB 1995]. And the Word became flesh and dwelt among men. As spoken by the prophets, He was called out of Egypt, raised a Nazarene, but born in Bethlehem. He learned obedience through His sufferings. Yet, He lived without sin, that He would be the perfect Lamb to cleanse the sins of man.

"HEAR OH ISREAL, THE LORD OUR GOD IS ONE, and you shall love the Lord your God with all your heart, mind, soul, and strength." He taught, "Love the Lord your God with all your heart, mind, soul, and strength; and, love your neighbor as yourself. No greater law than these". Crucify Him! We cried, crucify Him! We cannot bear His words, crucify Him cried – sinful man.

So, we took Him, stripped Him, and beat Him. We plucked His beard and scourged Him. Then, we nailed Him to that tree. Crowned with thorns we raised Him up for all the world to see. I spat toward Him and mocked Him and then, He prayed – for me. Six long hours, nailed to that cross, He suffered, bled, and died. To prove His death, I took my spear and pierced His body's side. Came forth blood and water, water and blood.

Mid-day, three hours since that darkness fell, the earth shook! Boulders broke! Torn was the holy veil. Tear this temple down. He had said, tear this temple down. "Tear this temple down and I will raise it on day three." Tear this temple down. Crucify Him --- Crucify Him.

Death could not hold the King of kings. Hell could not burn the Prince of peace. For, on the third day, He arose! Proclaiming victory, He led captive many captives and gave gifts unto men. Forty days with His disciples teaching more of His kingdom. By the hundreds could bear witness. We have seen Him, He arose! Then, He ascended to the Father who sent us the Holy Ghost.

He is the Alpha and Omega, the Beginning and the End, King of kings, Lord of lords, Prince of Peace, the Great I Am!, Root and Offspring of David, Juda's Lion, and The Lamb, Jesus Christ the risen Savior, Son of God and, Son of man.

Then He says, "I am He that's risen and was dead. Behold! I am alive forevermore. I have the keys of Hell and of Death. Behold! I am He that's risen and was dead".

He is the Alpha and Omega, the Beginning and the End, King of kings, Lord of lords, Prince of peace, the Great I Am!, Root and Offspring of David, Juda's Lion, and the Lamb. Jesus Christ the risen Savior, Son of God and Son of man; because, in the beginning was the Word: Jesus Christ the risen Savior, Son of God and Son of Man.

A compiling of scripture to better understand: Prose with footnotes

Translations used:

NAS New American Standard
KJV King James Version
AMP Amplified
CJB Complete Jewish Bible
NIV New International Version

"Who Is, This, Jesus?"

The Book of "Acts of the Apostles" -- chapter 2 -- The day of Pentecost. Thousands came to the Lord that day. Peter, addressing the multitude: "This Jesus whom you crucified -- by the hands of wicked men...". This was weeks after the crucifixion. Surely, most of those people were not there. As, neither were we. "This Jesus, whom YOU crucified by the hands of wicked men...". Nor were they before Pilot crying "Crucify Him! Crucify Him! Give us Barabbas! Crucify Jesus!" Again, neither were we. So, as is written in the Bible---Who is this Jesus whom WE crucified--- by the hands of wicked men?

(1) In the beginning was the Word. And the Word was with God. And the Word was God(a). All things were made through Him and without Him nothing was made that was made(b). And the Word became flesh and dwelt among men(c). As spoked by the prophets, He was called out of Egypt, raised a Nazarene, but born in Bethlehem(d). He learned obedience through His sufferings(e). Yet, He lived without sin(f) that He would be the perfect Lamb to cleanse the sins of man(g). 1 (a--Jn1:1) (b--Jn1:3) (c--Jn 1:14) (d-- Matt2:1,15,23) (e-- Heb 5:8 ; 2:10 ; 2:18) (f-- Heb 4:15; 1Jn 1:7) (g --Rev 1:5; Jn 1:29)

(2) " HEAR OH ISREAL, THE LORD OUR GOD IS ONE, and you shall love the Lord your God with all your heart, mind, soul, and strength." He taught, "Love the Lord your God with all your heart, mind, soul, and strength. And, love your neighbor as yourself. No greater law than these"(a). Crucify Him! We cried crucify Him! (b) We cannot bear His

11

words. Crucify Him, crucify Him, cried sinful man (c-1,2,3,4). 2 (a--Mark 12:29-31) (b--Matt 27:22) (c1—1 Jn 1:8) (c2—1 Jn 2:2) (c-3-- Ro 3:21-26) (c-4—James 2:10)

(3) So, we took Him, stripped Him, and beat Him(a). We plucked His beard and scourged Him(b). Then, we nailed Him to that tree(c). Crowned with thorns, we raised Him up for all the world to see(d,e). I spat toward Him and mocked Him(f). And then, He prayed--for me(g). Six long hours, nailed to that cross, He suffered, bled, and died(h). To prove His death, I took my spear and pierced His body's side. Came forth blood and water, water and blood(i). 3 (a-- Matt 27:28-30) (b-- Is 50:6) (c--Jn 19:1) (d-- Acts 2:23; 5:30) (e—Jn 19:1-3, 18; Matt 27: 38-42) (f-- Luke 18:32-33; Mark 15:16-20; Matt 27:30) (g--Luke 23:34) (h—Mark 15:25; 34-37) (i--Jn 19:34)

(4) Mid-day, three hours since that darkness fell, the earth shook! Boulders broke! Torn, was the holy veil(a,b). Tear this Temple down. He had said, tear this Temple down. "Tear this Temple down and I will raise it on day three"(c). Tear this Temple down. Crucify Him ---- crucify Him. 4 (a— Luke 23:44-45; Mark 15:33; Matt 27:45) (b—Mark 15:38; Matt27:50-51) (c—Matt 27:63; Jn 2:19)

(5) Death could not hold the King of kings.(a) Hell could not burn the Prince of Peace.(b) For on the third day He arose(c) proclaiming victory He led captive many captives and gave gifts unto men(d). Forty days with His disciples teaching more of His kingdom(e). By the hundreds could bare-witness. We have seen Him, He arose!(f) Then, He ascended to the Father,(g) who sent us the Holy Ghost!(h) 5 (a--Rev 17:14) (b--Eph 4:9; Is 9:6; Rev1:18; Acts 2:31) (c-- Acts 10:40; Jn 2:19 ; 1Cor 15:4) (d—Jn 14:26; Eph 4:8-13; Ro 12:6-8 ; 1 Cor 12:27-31; Acts 2:38-39) (e—Acts 1:3) (f—1 Cor 15:6) (g—Mark 16:19; Luke 24:50-51) (h—Luke 24:49; 1 Cor 12:3; Acts 2:38-39)

(6) He is the Alpha and Omega, the Beginning and the End, King of kings, Lord of lords, Prince of Peace(a,c), the Great I AM(d), Root and Offspring of David(e), Judah's Lion(f), and The LAMB(b,g). Jesus Christ the risen

Savior(g) Son of God and Son of man(h). 6 (a--Rev 1:8, 22:13, 21:6) (b--1Tim 6:14-16; Rev 17:14) (c-- Is 9:6) (d-- Jn 8:58) (e-- Rev 22:16) (f--Rev 5:5) (g--Jn 1:29) (h-- Ro 5:9-11, 15 ; Luke 22:69-70)

(7) Then, He says, "I am He that's risen and was dead. Behold, I am alive forever more. I have the keys of Hell and of Death. Behold! I am He that's risen and was dead." 7 (Rev 1:18; Jn 11:25)

(8) He is the Alpha and Omega, the Beginning, and the End, King of kings, Lord of lords, Prince of Peace, the Great I AM, Root and Offspring of David, Judah's Lion, and The LAMB, Jesus Christ the risen Savior, Son of God, and Son of man; because, in the beginning was the Word -- Jesus Christ the risen Savior, Son of God and Son of man. [6 & 8]; (Jn 1:1)

Scriptures for " Who Is,This, Jesus ?"

1 (a) Jn1:1

NASB --- In the beginning was the Word, and the Word was with God, and the Word was God.

AMP----- In the beginning [before all time] was the Word (Christ), and the Word was with God, and the Word was God Himself.

CJB------ In the beginning was the Word, and the Word was with God, and the Word was God.

KJV------ In the beginning was the Word, and the Word was with God, and the Word was God.

NIV------ In the beginning was the Word, and the Word was with God, and the Word was God.

1 (b) Jn1:3

NASB---- All things came into being through Him, and apart from Him nothing came into being that has come into being.

AMP----- All things were made and came into existence through Him; and without Him not even one thing was made that has come into being,

CJB------ All things came to be through him, and without him nothing made had being.

KJV....... All things were made by him; and without him was not anything made that was made.

NIV....... Through him all things were made; without him nothing was made that has been made.

1 (c) Jn 1: 14

NASB... And the Word became flesh, and dwelt among us, and we saw His glory, glory as of the only begotten from the Father, full of grace and truth.

AMP.... And the Word (Christ) became flesh, and lived among us; and we [actually] saw His glory, glory as belongs to the [One and] only begotten Son of the Father, [the Son who is truly unique, the only One of His kind, who is] full of grace and truth (absolutely free of deception).

CJB....... The Word became a human being and lived with us, and we saw his Sh'khinah, the Sh'khinah of the Father's only Son, full of grace and truth.

KJV....... And the Word was made flesh, and dwelt among us, (and we beheld his glory, the glory as of the only begotten of the Father,) full of grace and truth.

NIV....... The Word became flesh and made his dwelling among us. We have seen his glory, the glory of the one and only Son, who came from the Father, full of grace and truth.

1 (d-1) Matt 2:1

NASB...Now after Jesus was born in Bethlehem of Judea in the days of Herod the king, magi from the east arrived in Jerusalem, saying,

AMP.... Now when Jesus was born in Bethlehem of Judea in the days of Herod the king (Herod the Great), magi (wise men) from the east came to Jerusalem, asking,

CJB.......After Yeshua was born in Beit-Lechem in the land of Y'hudah during the time when Herod was king, Magi from the east came to Yerushalayim

KJV.......Now when Jesus was born in Bethlehem of Judaea in the days of Herod the king, behold, there came wise men from the east to Jerusalem,

NIV.......After Jesus was born in Bethlehem in Judea, during the time of King Herod, Magi from the east came to Jerusalem

1 (d-2) Matt 2:15

NASB... He remained there until the death of Herod. This was to fulfill what had been spoken by the Lord through the prophet: "out of Egypt I called my son."

AMP.... He remained there until the death of Herod. This was to fulfill what the Lord had spoken by the prophet [Hosea]: "Out of Egypt I called My Son."

CJB...... where he stayed until Herod died. This happened in order to fulfill what Adonai had said through the prophet, "Out of Egypt I called my son."

KJV...... And was there until the death of Herod: that it might be fulfilled which was spoken of the Lord by the prophet, saying, Out of Egypt have I called my son.

NIV...... where he stayed until the death of Herod. And so was fulfilled what the Lord had said through the prophet: "Out of Egypt I called my son."

1 (d-3) Matt 2:23

NASB... and came and lived in a city called Nazareth. This was to fulfill what was spoken through the prophets: "He shall be called a Nazarene."

AMP.... and went and settled in a city called Nazareth. This was to fulfill what was spoken through the prophets: "He shall be called a Nazarene."

CJB....... and settled in a town called Natzeret, so that what had been spoken by the prophets might be fulfilled, that he will be called a Natzrati.

KJV.......And he came and dwelt in a city called Nazareth: that it might be fulfilled which was spoken by the prophets, He shall be called a Nazarene.

NIV.... and he went and lived in a town called Nazareth. So was fulfilled what was said through the prophets, that he would be called a Nazarene.

1 (e-1) Heb 5:8

NASB... Although He was a Son, He learned obedience from the things which He suffered.

AMP.... Although He was a Son [who had never been disobedient to the Father], He learned [active, special] obedience through what He suffered.

CJB...... Even though he was the Son, he learned obedience through his sufferings.

KJV.......Though he were a Son, yet learned he obedience by the things which he suffered;

NIV....... Son though he was, he learned obedience from what he suffered

1 (e-2) Heb 2:10

NASB...For it was fitting for Him, for whom are all things, and through whom are all thing, in bringing many sons to glory, to perfect the author of their salvation through sufferings.

AMP....For it was fitting for God [that is, an act worthy of His divine nature] that He, for whose sake are all things, and through whom are all things, in bringing many sons to glory should make the author and founder of their salvation perfect through suffering [bringing to maturity the human experience necessary for Him to be perfectly equipped for His office as High Priest].

CJB....... For in bringing many sons to glory, it was only fitting that God, the Creator and Preserver of everything, should bring the Initiator of their deliverance to the goal through sufferings.

KJV....... For it became him, for whom are all things, and by whom are all things, in bringing many sons unto glory, to make the captain of their salvation perfect through sufferings.

NIV....... In bringing many sons and daughters to glory, it was fitting that God, for whom and through whom everything exists, should make the pioneer of their salvation perfect through what he suffered.

1 (e-3) Heb: 2:18

NASB... For since He Himself was tempted in that which He has suffered, He is able to come to the aid of those who are tempted.

AMP.... Because He Himself [in His humanity] has suffered in being tempted, He is able to help and provide immediate assistance to those who are being tempted and exposed to suffering.

CJB....... For since he himself suffered death when he was put to the test, he is able to help those who are being tested now.

KJV........ For in that he himself hath suffered being tempted, he is able to succour them that are tempted.

NIV....... Because he himself suffered when he was tempted, he is able to help those who are being tempted.

1 (f-1) Heb 4:15

NASB... For we do not have a high priest who cannot sympathize with our weaknesses, but One who has been tempted in all things as we are, yet without sin.

AMP.... For we do not have a High Priest who is unable to sympathize and understand our weaknesses and temptations, but One who has been tempted [knowing exactly how it feels to be human] in every respect as we are, yet without [committing any] sin.

CJB...... For we do not have a cohen gadol unable to empathize with our weaknesses; since in every respect tempted just as we are, the only difference being that he did not sin.

KJV...... For we have not an high priest which cannot be touched with the feeling of our infirmities; but was in all points tempted like as we are, yet without sin.

NIV....... For we do not have a high priest who is unable to empathize with our weaknesses, but we have one who has been tempted in every way, just as we are -- yet he did not sin.

1 (f-2) 1 Jn 1:7

NASB... but if we walk in the Light as He Himself is in the Light, we have fellowship with one another, and the blood of Jesus His Son cleanses us from all sin.

AMP.... but if we [really] walk in the Light [that is, live each and every day in conformity with the precepts of God], as He Himself is in the Light, we have [true, unbroken] fellowship with one another [He with us, and we with Him], and the blood of Jesus His Son cleanses us from all sin [by erasing the stain of sin, keeping us cleansed from sin in all its forms and manifestations].

CJB...... But if we are walking in the light, as he is in the light, then we have fellowship with each other, and the blood of his Son Yeshua purifies us from all sin.

KJV...... But if we walk in the light, as he is in the light, we have fellowship one with another, and the blood of Jesus Christ his Son cleanseth us from all sin.

NIV...... But if we walk in the light, as he is in the light, we have fellowship with one another, and the blood of Jesus, his Son, purifies us from all sin.

1 (g-1) Rev 1:5

NASB... and from Jesus Christ, the faithful witness, the firstborn of the dead, and the ruler of the kings of the earth. To Him who loves us and released us from our sins by His blood--

AMP....... and from Jesus Christ, the faithful and trustworthy Witness, the Firstborn of the dead, and the Ruler of the kings of the earth. To Him who [always] loves us and who [has once for all] freed us [or washed us] from our sins by His own blood (His sacrificial death)--

CJB....... and from Yeshua the Messiah, the faithful witness, the firstborn from the dead and the ruler of the earth's kings. To him, the one who loves us, who has freed us from our sins at the cost of his blood,

KJV....... And from Jesus Christ, who is the faithful witness, and the first begotten of the dead, and the prince of the kings of the earth. Unto him that loved us, and washed us from our sins in his own blood,

21

NIV....... and from Jesus Christ, who is the faithful witness, the firstborn from the dead, and the ruler of the kings of the earth. To him who loves us and has freed us from our sins by his blood,

1 (g-2) Jn1:29

NASB...The next day he saw Jesus coming to him and said, "Behold, the Lamb of God who takes away the sin of the world!

AMP.... The next day he saw Jesus coming to him and said, "Look! The Lamb of God who takes away the sin of the world!

CJB....... The next day, Yochanan saw Yeshua coming toward him and said, "Look! God's lamb! the one who is taking away the sin of the world!

KJV....... The next day John seeth Jesus coming unto him, and saith, Behold the Lamb of God, which taketh away the sin of the world.

NIV....... The next day John saw Jesus coming toward him and said, "Look, the Lamb of God, who takes away the sin of the world!

2 (a) Mark12: 29-31

NASB...Jesus answered, "The foremost is, 'Hear, O Israel! The Lord our God is one Lord; and you shall love the Lord your God with all your heart, and with all your soul, and with all your mind, and with all your strength. The second is this, 'you shall love your neighbor as yourself'. There is no other commandment greater than these."

AMP....Jesus answered, "The first and most important one is: 'Hear, O Israel, the Lord our God is one Lord; and you shall love the Lord your God with all your heart, and with all your soul (life), and with all your mind (thought, understanding), and with all your strength.' This is the second: 'You shall [unselfishly] love your neighbor as yourself.' There is no other commandment greater than these."

CJB......Yeshua answered, "The most important is, ' Sh'ma Yisra'el, Adonai Eloheinu, Adonai echad [Hear, O Isra'el, the Lord our God, the Lord is one], and you are to love Adonai your God with all your heart, with all your soul, with all your understanding and with all your strength.' The second is this: You are to love your neighbor as yourself.' There is no other mitzvah greater than these."

KJV......And Jesus answered him, "The first of all the commandments is, Hear, O Israel; The lord our God is one Lord: And thou shalt love the Lord thy God with all thy heart, and with all thy soul, and with all thy mind, and with all thy strength: this is the first commandment. And the second is like, namely this, Thou shalt love thy neighbor as thyself. There is none other commandment greater than these.

NIV......"The most important one," answered Jesus, "is this: 'Hear, O Israel: The Lord our God, the Lord is one. Love the Lord your God with all your heart and with all your soul and with all your mind and with all your strength.' The second is this: 'Love your neighbor as yourself.' There is no commandment greater than these."

2 (b) Matt27 : 22

NASB... Pilate said to them, "Then what shall I do with Jesus who is called Christ?" They all said "Crucify Him!"

AMP.... Pilate said to them, "Then what shall I do with Jesus who is called Christ?" They all replied, "Let Him be crucified!"

CJB...... Pilate said to them, "Then what should I do with Yeshua, called 'the Messiah'?" They all said, "Put him to death on the stake! Put him to death on the stake!"

KJV...... Pilate saith unto them, What shall I do then with Jesus which is called Christ? They all say unto him, Let him be crucified.

NIV...... "What shall I do, then, with Jesus who is called the Messiah?" Pilate asked. They all answered, "Crucify him!"

2 (c-1) 1 Jn 1: 8

NASB... If we say that we have no sin, we are deceiving ourselves and the truth is not in us.

AMP.... If we say we have no sin [refusing to admit that we are sinners], we delude ourselves and the truth is not in us. [His word does not live in our hearts.]

CJB...... If we claim not to have sin, we are deceiving ourselves, and the truth is not in us.

KJV...... If we say that we have no sin, we deceive ourselves, and the truth is not in us.

NIV...... If we claim to be without sin, we deceive ourselves and the truth is not in us.

2 (c-2) 1 Jn 2: 2

NASB... and He Himself is the propitiation for our sins; and not for ours only, but also for those of the whole world.

AMP.... And He [that same Jesus] is the propitiation for our sins [the atoning sacrifice that holds back the wrath of God that would otherwise be directed at us because of our sinful nature -- our worldliness, our lifestyle]; and not for ours alone, but also for [the sins of all believers throughout] the whole world.

CJB...... Also, He is the kapparah for our sins -- and not only for ours, but also for those of the whole world.

KJV...... And he is the propitiation for our sins: and not for ours only, but also for the sins of the whole world.

NIV...... He is the atoning sacrifice for our sins, and not only for ours but also for the sins of the whole world.

2 (c-3) Ro 3: 21-26

NASB... But now apart from the Law the righteousness of God has been manifested, being witnessed by the Law and the Prophets, even the righteousness of God through faith in Jesus Christ for all those who believe; for there is no distinction; for all have sinned and fall short of the glory of God, being justified as a gift by His grace through the redemption which is in Christ Jesus; whom God displayed publicly as a propitiation in His blood through faith. This was to demonstrate His righteousness, because in the forbearance of God He passed over the sins previously committed; for the demonstration, I say, of His righteousness at the present time, so that He would be just and the justifier of the one who has faith in Jesus.

AMP.... But now the righteousness of God has been clearly revealed [independently and completely] apart from the Law, though it is [actually] confirmed by the Law and the [words and writings of the] Prophets. This righteousness of God comes through faith in Jesus Christ for all those [Jew or Gentile] who believe [and trust in Him and acknowledge Him as God's Son]. There is no distinction, since all have sinned and continually fall short of the glory of God, and are being justified [declared free of the guilt of sin, made acceptable to God, and granted eternal life] as a gift by His [precious, undeserved] grace, through the redemption [the payment for our sin] which is [provided] in Christ Jesus, whom God displayed publicly [before the eyes of the world] as a [life-giving] sacrifice of atonement and reconciliation (propitiation) by His blood [to be received] through faith. This was to demonstrate His righteousness [which demands punishment for sin], because in His forbearance [His deliberate restraint] He passed over the sins previously committed [before Jesus' crucifixion]. It was to demonstrate His righteousness at the present time, so that He would be

25

just and the One who justifies those who have faith in Jesus [and rely confidently...

CJB...... But now, quite apart from Torah, God's way of making people righteous in his sight has been made clear -- although the Torah and the Prophets give their witness to it as well -- and it is a righteousness that comes from God, through the faithfulness of Yeshua the Messiah, to all who continue trusting. For it makes no difference whether one is a Jew or a Gentile, since all have sinned and come short of earning God's praise. By God's grace, without earning it, all are granted the status of being considered righteous before him, through the act redeeming us from our enslavement to sin that was accomplished by the Messiah Yeshua. God put Yeshua forward as the kapparah for sin through his faithfulness in respect to his bloody sacrificial death. This vindicated God's righteousness; because, in his forbearance, he had passed over [with neither punishment nor remission] the sins people had committed in the past; and it vindicates his righteousness in the present age by showing that he is righteous himself and is also the one who makes people righteous on the ground of Yeshua's faithfulness.

KJV...... But now the righteousness of God without the law is manifested, being witnessed by the law and the prophets; Even the righteousness of God which is by faith of Jesus Christ unto all and upon all them that believe: for there is no difference: For all have sinned, and come short of the glory of God; Being justified freely by his grace through the redemption that is in Christ Jesus: Whom God hath set forth to be a propitiation through faith in his blood, to declare his righteousness for the remission of sins that are past, through the forbearance of God; To declare, I say, at this time his righteousness: that he might be just, and the justifier of him which believeth in Jesus.

NIV...... But now apart from the law the righteousness of God has been made known, to which the Law and the Prophets testify. This righteousness is given through faith in Jesus Christ to all who believe. There is no difference between Jew and Gentile, for all have sinned and fall short of the glory of God, and all are justified freely by his grace through the redemption that came by Christ Jesus. God presented Christ as a sacrifice of atonement, through the shedding of his blood --to be received by faith. He did this to demonstrate his righteousness, because in his forbearance he had left the sins committed beforehand unpunished -- he did it to demonstrate his righteousness at the present time, so as to be just and the one who justifies those who have faith in Jesus.

2 (c-4) James 2:10

NASB...For whoever keeps the whole law and yet stumbles in one point, he has become guilty of all.

AMP....For whoever keeps the whole Law but stumbles in one point, he has become guilty of [breaking] all of it.

CJB......For a person who keeps the whole Torah, yet stumbles at one point, has become guilty of breaking them all.

KJV......For whosoever shall keep the whole law, and yet offend in one point, he is guilty of all.

NIV......For whoever keeps the whole law and yet stumbles at just one point is guilty of breaking all of it.

3 (a) Matt 27: 28-31

NASB... They stripped Him and put a scarlet robe on Him. And after twisting together a crown of thorns, they put it on His head, and a reed in His right hand; and they knelt down before Him and mocked Him, saying, "Hail, King of the Jews!" They spat on Him, and took the reed and began to beat Him on the head. After they had mocked Him, they took the scarlet robe off Him and put His own garments back on Him, and led Him away to crucify Him.

AMP.....They stripped him and put a scarlet robe on Him [as a king's robe]. And after twisting together a crown of thorns, they put it on His head, and put a reed in His right hand [as a scepter]. Kneeling before Him, they ridiculed Him, saying, "Hail (rejoice), King of the Jews!" They spat on Him, and took the reed and struck Him repeatedly on the head. After they finished ridiculing Him, they stripped Him of the scarlet robe and put His own clothes on Him, and led Him away to crucify Him.

CJB......They stripped off his clothes and put on him a scarlet robe, wove thorn-branches into a crown and put it on his head, and put a stick in his right hand. Then they kneeled down in front of him and made fun of him: "Hail to the King of the Jews!" They spit on him and used the stick to beat him about the head. When they had finished ridiculing him, they took off the robe, put his own clothes back on him and led him away to be nailed to the execution-stake.

KJV....... And they stripped him, and put on him a scarlet robe. And when they had platted a crown of thorns, they put it upon his head, and a reed in his right hand: and they bowed the knee before him and mocked him, saying, Hail, King of the Jews! And they spit upon him, and took the reed, and smote him on the head. And after that they had mocked him, they took the robe off from him, and put his own raiment on him, and led him away to crucify him.

NIV....... They stripped him and put a scarlet robe on him, and then twisted together a crown of thorns and set it on his head. They put a staff in his right hand. Then they knelt in front of him and mocked him. "Hail, king of the Jews!" they said, They spit on him, and took the staff and struck him on the head again and again. After they had mocked him, they took off the robe and put his own clothes on him. Then they led him away to crucify him.

3 (b) Is 50: 6

NASB... I gave My back to those who strike Me, And My cheeks to those who pluck out the beard; I did not cover My face from humiliation and spitting.

AMP.... I turned My back to those who strike Me, And My cheeks to those who pluck out the beard; I did not hide My face from insults and spitting.

CJB...... I offered by back to those who struck me, my cheeks to those who plucked out my beard; I did not hide my face from insult and spitting.

KJV...... I gave my back to the smiters, and my cheeks to them that plucked off the hair: I hid not my face from shame and spitting,

NIV....... I offered my back to those who beat me, my cheeks to those who pulled out my beard; I did not hide my face from mocking and spitting.

3 (c-1) Jn 19: 1

NASB... Pilate then took Jesus and scourged Him.

AMP.... So then Pilate took Jesus and had Him scourged (flogged, whipped).

CJB....... Pilate then took Yeshua and had him flogged.

KJV....... Then Pilate therefore took Jesus, and scourged him.

NIV....... Then Pilate took Jesus and had him flogged.

3 (d-1) Acts 2: 23

NASB... this Man, delivered over by the predetermined plan and foreknowledge of God, you nailed to a cross by the hands of godless men and put Him to death.

AMP.... this Man, when handed over [to the Roman authorities] according to the predetermined decision and foreknowledge of God, you nailed to a cross and put to death by the hands of lawless and godless men.

CJB....... This man was arrested in accordance with God's predetermined plan and foreknowledge; and, through the agency of persons not bound by the Torah, you nailed him up on a stake and killed him!

KJV....... Him, being delivered by the determinate counsel and foreknowledge of God, ye have taken, and by wicked hands have crucified and slain:

NIV....... This man was handed over to you by God's deliberate plan and foreknowledge; and you, with the help of wicked men, put him to death by nailing him to the cross.

3(d-2) Acts 5: 30

NASB... The God of our fathers raised up Jesus, whom thou had put to death by hanging Him on a cross.

AMP.... The God of our fathers raised up Jesus, whom you had put to death by hanging Him on a cross [and you are responsible].

CJB....... The God of our fathers raised up Yeshua where as you men killed him by having him hanged on a stake.

KJV....... The God of our fathers raised up Jesus, whom ye slew and hanged on a tree

NIV...... The God of our ancestors raised Jesus from the dead -- whom you killed by hanging him on a cross.

3 (e-1) Jn 19:1-3

NASB...Pilot then took Jesus and scourged Him. And the soldiers twisted together a crown of thorns and put it on His head, and put a purple robe on Him; and they began to come up to Him and say, "Hail, King of the Jews!" and to give Him slaps in the face.

AMP....So then Pilate took Jesus and had Him scourged (flogged, whipped). And the soldiers twisted together a crown of thorns and put it on His head, and put a purple robe around Him, and they kept coming up to Him, saying [mockingly], "Hail, King of the Jews [Good health! Peace! Long life to you, King of the Jews]!" And they slapped Him in the face.

CJB......Pilate then took Yeshua and had him flogged. The soldiers twisted thorn-branches into a crown and placed it on his head, put a purple robe on him, and went up to him, saying over and over, "Hail, 'king of the Jews'!" and hitting him in the face.

KJV.......Then Pilate therefore took Jesus, and scourged him. And the soldiers platted a crown of thorns, and put it on his head, and they put on him a purple robe, And said, Hail, King of the Jews! and they smote him with their hands.

NIV.......Then Pilate took Jesus and had him flogged. The soldiers twisted together a crown of thorns and put it on his head. They clothed him in a purple robe and went up to him again and again, saying, "Hail, king of the Jews!" And they slapped him in the face.

3 (e-2) Jn 19: 18

NASB... There they crucified Him, and with Him two other men, one on either side, and Jesus in between.

AMP.... There they crucified Him, and with Him two others, one on either side, and Jesus between them.

CJB.......There they nailed him to the stake along with two others, one on either side, with Yeshua in the middle.

KJV....... Where they crucified him, and two other with him, on either side one, and Jesus in the midst.

NIV....... There they crucified him, and with him two others--one on each side and Jesus in the middle.

3 (e-3) Matt 27: 38 - 42

NASB... At that time two robbers were crucified with Him, one on the right and one on the left. And those passing by were hurling abuse at Him, wagging their heads and saying, "You who are going to destroy the temple and rebuild it in three days, save Yourself! If You are the Son of God, come down from the cross." In the same way the chief priests also, along with the scribes and elders, were mocking Him and saying, "He saved others; He cannot save Himself. He is the King of Israel; let Him now come down from the cross, and we will believe in Him.

AMP.... At the same time two robbers were crucified with Jesus, one on the right and one on the left. Those who passed by were hurling abuse at Him and jeering at Him, wagging their heads [in scorn and ridicule], and they said [tauntingly], "You who would destroy the temple and rebuild it in three days, save Yourself [from death]! If you are the Son of God, come down from the cross." In the same way the chief priests also, along with the scribes and elders, mocked Him, saying, "He saved others [from death]; He cannot save Himself. He is the King of Israel; let Him now come down from the cross, and we will believe in Him and acknowledge Him.

CJB.......Then two robbers were placed on execution-stakes with him, one on the right and one on the left. People passing by hurled insults at him, shaking their heads and saying, "So you can destroy the Temple, can you, and rebuild it in three days? Save yourself, if you are the Son of God, and come down from the stake!" Likewise, the head cohanim jeered at him, along with the Torah-teachers and elders, "He saved others, but he can't save himself!" "So he's King of Isra'el, is he? Let him come down now from the stake! Then we'll believe him!"

KJV....... Then were there two thieves crucified with him, one on the right hand, and another on the left. And they that passed by reviled him, wagging their heads, and saying, Thou that destroyest the temple, and buildest it in three days, save thyself. If thou be the Son of God, come down from the cross. Likewise also the chief priests mocking him, with the scribes and elders, said, He saved others; himself he cannot save. If he be the King of Israel, let him now come down from the cross, and we will believe him.

NIV....... Two rebels were crucified with him, one on his right and one on his left. Those who passed by hurled insults at him, shaking their heads and saying, "You who are going to destroy the temple and build it in three days, save yourself! Come down from the cross, if you are the Son of God!" In the same way the chief priests, the teachers of the law and the elders mocked him. "He saved others," they said, "but he can't save himself! He's the king of Israel! Let him come down now from the cross, and we will believe in him.

3 (f-1) Luke 18: 32 - 33

NASB...For He will be handed over to the Gentiles, and will be mocked and mistreated and spit upon, and after they have scourged Him, they will kill Him; and the third day He will rise again.

AMP.... He will be betrayed and handed over to the Gentiles (Roman authorities), and will be mocked and ridiculed and insulted and abused and spit on, and after they have scourged Him, they will kill Him; and on the third day He will rise [from the dead].

CJB....... For he will be handed over to the Gayim and be ridiculed, insulted, and spat upon. Then after they have beaten him, they will kill him. But on the third day he will rise.

KJV....... For he shall be delivered unto the Gentiles, and shall be mocked, and spitefully entreated, and spitted on: And they shall scourge him. and put him to death: and the third day he shall rise again.

NIV.... For he shall be delivered unto the Gentiles. They will mock him, insult him and spit on him; they will flog him and kill him. On the third day he will rise again.

3 (f-2) Mark 15: 16 - 20

NASB... The soldiers took Him away into the palace (that is the Praetorium), and they called together the whole Roman cohort. They dressed Him up in purple, and after twisting a crown of thorns, they put it on Him, and they began to acclaim Him "Hail, King of the Jews!" They kept beating His head with a reed, and spitting on Him, and kneeling and bowing before Him. After they had mocked Him, they took the purple robe off Him and put His own garments on Him. And they led Him out to crucify Him.

AMP.... The soldiers led Him away into the palace (that is, the Praetorium), and they called together the entire [Roman} battalion [of 600 soldiers]. They dressed Him up in [a ranking Roman officer's robe of] purple, and after twisting [together] a crown of thorns, they placed it on Him; and they began saluting and mocking Him "Hail, King of the Jews!" They kept beating Him on the head with a reed and spitting on Him, and kneeling and bowing in [mock] homage to Him. After they had mocked Him, they took off the purple robe and put His own clothes on Him. And they led Him out [of the city] to crucify Him.

CJB....... The soldiers led him away inside the palace (that is, the headquarters building) and called together the whole battalion. They dressed him in purple and wove thorn branches into a crown, which they put on him. Then they began to salute him, "Hail to the King of the Jews!" They hit him on the head with a stick, spat on him and kneeled in mock worship of him. When they had finished ridiculing him, they took off the purple robe, put his own clothes back on him and led him away to be nailed to the execution-stake.

KJV...... And the soldiers led him away into the hall, called Praetorium; and they called together the whole band. And they clothed him with purple, and platted a crown of thorns, and put it about his head, and began to salute him "Hail, King of the Jews!" And they smote him on the head with a reed, and did spit upon him, and bowing their knees worshipped him. And when they had mocked him, they took off the purple from him, and put his own clothes on him, and led him out to crucify him.

NIV...... The soldiers led Jesus away into the palace (that is, the Praetorium) and called together the whole company of soldiers. They put a purple robe on him, they twisted together a crown of thorns and set it on him. And they began to call out to him "Hail, king of the Jews!" Again and again, they struck him on the head with a staff and spit on him. Falling on their knees, they paid homage to him. And when they had mocked him, they took off the purple robe and put his own clothes on him. Then they led him out to crucify him.

3 (f-3) Matt 27: 30

NASB...They spat on Him, and took the reed and began to beat Him on the head.

AMP....They spat on Him, and took the reed and struck Him repeatedly on the head.

CJB......They spit on him and used the stick to beat him about the head.

KJV......And they spit upon him, and took the reed, and smote him on the head.

NIV......They spit on him, and took the staff and struck him on the head again and again.

3 (g) Luke 23: 34

NASB... But Jesus was saying, "Father, forgive them; for they do not know what they are doing." And they cast lots, dividing up His garments among themselves.

AMP.... And Jesus was saying, "Father, forgive them; for they do not know what they are doing." And they cast lots, dividing His clothes among themselves.

CJB....... Yeshua said, "Father, forgive them; they don't understand what they are doing." They divided up his clothes by throwing dice.

KJV....... Then said Jesus, Father, forgive them; for they know not what they do. And they parted his raiment, and cast lots.

NIV....... Jesus said, "Father, forgive them, for they do not know what they are doing." And they divided up his clothes by casting lots.

3 (h-1) Mark 15: 25

NASB... It was the third hour when they crucified Him.

AMP.... It was the third hour (9:00 a.m.) when they crucified Him.

CJB....... It was nine in the morning when they nailed him to the stake.

KJV....... And it was the third hour, and they crucified him.

NIV....... It was nine in the morning when they crucified him.

3 (h-2) Mark 15: 34 - 37

NASB... At the ninth hour Jesus cried out with a loud voice, "ELOI, ELOI, LAMA SABACHTHANI?" which is translated, MY GOD, MY GOD, WHY HAVE YOU FORSAKEN ME?" When some of the bystanders heard it, they began saying, "Behold, He is calling for Elijah." Someone ran and filled a sponge with sour wine, put it on a reed, and gave Him a drink, saying, "Let us see whether Elijah will come to take Him down." And Jesus uttered a loud cry, and breathed His last.

AMP.... And at the ninth hour Jesus cried out with a loud voice, "ELOI, ELOI, LAMA SABACHTHANI?" Some of the bystanders heard Him and said, "Look! He is calling for Elijah!" Someone ran and filled a sponge with sour wine, put it on a reed and gave Him a drink, saying, "Let us see whether Elijah is coming to take Him down." But Jesus uttered a loud cry, and breathed out His last [voluntarily, sovereignly dismissed and releasing His spirit from His body in submission to His Father's plan].

CJB....... At three, he uttered a loud cry, "Elohi! Elohi! L'mah sh'vaktani?" (which means, "My God! My God! Why have you deserted me?") On hearing this, some of the bystanders said, "Look! He's calling for Eliyahu!" One ran and soaked a sponge in vinegar, put it on a stick and gave it to him to drink. "Wait!" he said, "Let's see if Eliyahu will come and take him down." But Yeshua let out a loud cry and gave up his spirit.

KJV....... And at the ninth hour Jesus cried with a loud voice, saying, Eloi, Eloi, Lama sabachthani? which is, being interpreted, My God, my God, why hast thou forsaken me? And some of them that stood by, when they heard it, said, Behold, he calleth Elias. And one ran and filled a sponge full of vinegar, and put it on a reed, and gave him to drink, saying, Let alone; let us see whether Elias will come to take him down. And Jesus cried with a loud voice, and gave up the ghost.

NIV....... And at three in the afternoon Jesus cried out in a loud voice, "Eloi, Eloi lema sabachthani? (which means "My God, my God, why have you forsaken me?") When some of those standing near heard this, they said, "Listen, he's calling Elijah". Someone ran, filled a sponge with wine vinegar, put it on a staff, and offered it to Jesus to drink. "Now leave him alone. Let's see if Elijah comes to take him down," he said. With a loud cry, Jesus breathed his last.

3 (i) Jn 19 :34

NASB... But one of the soldiers pierced His side with a spear, and immediately blood and water came out.

AMP.... But one of the soldiers pierced His side with a spear, and immediately blood and water came [flowing] out.

CJB...... However, one of the soldiers stabbed his side with a spear, and at once blood and water flowed out.

KJV...... But one of the soldiers with a spear pierced his side, and forthwith came there out blood and water.

NIV...... Instead, one of the soldiers pierced Jesus' side with a spear, bringing a sudden flow of blood and water.

4(a-1) Luke 23: 44 - 45

NASB... It was now about the sixth hour, and darkness fell over the whole land until the ninth hour, because the sun was obscured; and the veil of the temple was torn in two.

AMP .... It was now about the sixth hour (noon). and darkness came over the whole land until the ninth hour (3:00 p.m.), because the sun was obscured; and the veil [of the Holy of Holies] of the temple was torn in two [from top to bottom].

CJB...... It was now about noon, and darkness covered the whole Land until three o'clock in the afternoon; the sun did not shine. Also the parokhet in the Temple was split down the middle.

KJV...... And it was about the sixth hour, and there was a darkness over all the earth until the ninth hour. And the sun was darkened, and the veil of the temple was rent in the midst.

NIV...... It was now about noon, and darkness came over the whole land until three in the afternoon, for the sun stopped shining. And the curtain of the temple was torn in two.

4 (a-2) Mark 15: 33

NASB... When the sixth hour came, darkness fell over the whole land until the ninth hour.

AMP.... When the sixth hour (noon) came, darkness covered the whole land until the ninth hour (3:00 p.m.)

CJB...... At noon, darkness covered the whole Land until three o'clock in the afternoon.

KJV...... And when the sixth hour was come, there was darkness over the whole land until the ninth hour.

NIV....... At noon, darkness came over the whole land until three in the afternoon.

4(a-3) Matt 27: 45

NASB... Now from the sixth hour darkness fell upon all the land until the ninth hour.

AMP.... Now from the sixth hour (noon) there was darkness over all the land until the ninth hour (3:00 p.m.)

CJB....... From noon until three o'clock in the afternoon, all the Land was covered with darkness.

KJV....... Now from the sixth hour there was darkness over all the land unto the ninth hour.

NIV....... From noon until three in the afternoon darkness came over all the land.

4 (b-1) Mark 15: 38

NASB... And the veil of the temple was torn in two from top to bottom.

AMP.... And the veil [of the Holy of Holies] of the temple was torn in two from top to bottom.

CJB....... And the parokhet in the Temple was torn in two from top to bottom.

KJV....... And the veil of the temple was rent in twain from the top to the bottom.

NIV....... The curtain of the temple was torn in two from top to bottom.

4 (b-2) Matt 27: 50 - 51

NASB... And Jesus cried out again with a loud voice, and yielded up His spirit. And behold, the veil of the temple was torn in two from top to bottom; and the earth shook and the rocks were split.

AMP.... And Jesus cried out again with a loud [agonized] voice, and gave up His spirit [voluntarily, sovereignly dismissing and releasing His spirit from His body in submission to His Father's plan]. And [at once] the veil [of the Holy of Holies] of the temple was torn in two from top to bottom; the earth shook and the rocks were split apart.

CJB...... But Yeshua, again crying out in a loud voice, yielded up his spirit. At that moment the parokhet in the Temple was ripped in two from top to bottom; and there was an earthquake, with rocks splitting apart.

KJV...... Jesus, when he had cried again with a loud voice, yielded up the ghost. And, behold, the veil of the temple was rent in twain from the top to the bottom; and the earth did quake, and the rocks rent;

NIV....... And when Jesus had cried out again in a loud voice, he gave up his spirit. At that moment the curtain of the temple was torn in two from top to bottom. The earth shook, the rocks split

4 (c-1) Matt 27: 63

NASB... (Pharisees) and said, "Sir, we remember that when He was still alive that deceiver said, 'After three days I am to rise again.

AMP.... and said, "Sir, we have remembered that when He was still alive that deceiver said, 'After three days I will rise [from the dead].'

CJB....... and said, "Sir, we remember that that deceiver said while he was still alive, 'After three days I will be raised.'

KJV....... Saying, Sir, we remember that that deceiver said, while he was yet alive, "After three days I will rise again.

NIV....... "Sir," they said, "we remember that while he was still alive that deceiver said, 'After three days I will rise again.'

4 (c-2) Jn 2: 19

NASB... Jesus answered them, "Destroy this temple, and in three days I will raise it up."

AMP.... Jesus answered them, "Destroy this temple, and in three days I will raise it up."

CJB....... Yeshua answered them, "Destroy this temple, and in three days I will raise it up again."

KJV....... Jesus answered and said unto them, Destroy this temple, and in three days I will raise it up.

NIV...... Jesus answered them, "Destroy this temple, and I will raise it again in three days."

5 (a-1) Rev 17: 14

NASB... These will wage war against the Lamb, and the Lamb will overcome them, because He is Lord of Lords and King of kings, and those who are with Him are the called and chosen and faithful."

AMP.... They will wage war against the Lamb (Christ), and the Lamb will triumph and conquer them, because He is Lord of Lords and King of kings, and those who are with Him and on His side are the called and chosen (elect) and faithful."

CJB....... They will go to war against the Lamb, but the Lamb will defeat them, because he is Lord of Lords and King of kings, and those who are called, chosen and faithful will overcome along with him."

KJV....... These shall make war with the Lamb, and the Lamb shall overcome them: for he is Lord of Lords, and King of kings: and they that are with him are called, and chosen, and faithful.

NIV....... They will wage war against the Lamb, but the Lamb will triumph over them because he is Lord of Lords and King of kings -- and with him will be his called, chosen and faithful."

5 (b-1) Eph 4: 9

NASB... (Now this expression, "He ascended," what does it mean except that He also had descended into the lower parts off the earth?

AMP.... (Now this expression, "He ascended," what does it mean except that He also had previously descended [from the heights of heaven] into the lower parts of the earth?

CJB...... Now this phrase, "he went up," what can it mean if not that he first went down into the lower parts, that is, the earth?

KJV....... (Now that he ascended, what is it but that he also descended first into the lower parts of the earth?

NIV....... (What does "he ascended" mean except that he also descended into the lower, earthly regions?

5 (b-2) Is 9: 6

NASB... For a child will be born to us, a son will be given to us; And the government will rest of His shoulders; And His name will be called Wonderful Counselor, Mighty God, Eternal Father, Prince of Peace.

AMP.... For to us a Child shall be born, to us a Son shall be given; And the government shall be upon His shoulder, And His name shall be called Wonderful Counselor, Mighty God, Everlasting Father, Prince of Peace.

CJB....... [vs. 5] For a child is born to us, a son is given to us; dominion will rest on his shoulders, and he will be given the name Pele-Yo'etz El Gibbor Avi-'Ad Sar-Shalom [Wonder of a Counselor, Mighty God, Father of Eternity, Prince of Peace],

KJV....... For unto us a child is born, unto us a son is given: and the government shall be upon his shoulder: and his name shall be called Wonderful, Counsellor, The mighty God, The everlasting Father, The Prince of Peace.

NIV...... For to us a child is born, to us a son is given, and the government will be on his shoulders. And he will be called Wonderful Counselor, Mighty God, Everlasting Father, Prince of Peace.

5 (b-3) Rev 1: 18

NASB... and the living One; and I was dead, and behold, I am alive forevermore, and I have the keys of death and of Hades.

AMP.... and the Ever-living One [living in and beyond all time and space]. I died, but see, I am alive forevermore, and I have the keys of [absolute control and victory over] death and of Hades (the realm of the dead).

CJB....... the Living One. I was dead, but look! -- I am alive forever and ever!.. And I hold the keys to Death and Sh'ol.

KJV....... I am he that liveth, and was dead; and, behold, I am alive for evermore, Amen; and have the keys of hell and of death.

NIV....... I am the Living One; I was dead, and now look, I am alive for ever and ever! And I hold the keys of death and Hades.

5 (b-4) Acts 2:31

NASB... he (David) looked ahead and spoke of the resurrection of the Christ, that He was neither abandoned to Hades, nor did His flesh suffer decay.

AMP.... he foresaw and spoke [prophetically] of the resurrection of the Christ (the Messiah, the Anointed), that He was not abandoned {in death} to Hades (the realm of the dead), nor did his body undergo decay.

CJB....... he was speaking in advance about the resurrection of the Messiah, that it was he who was not abandoned in Sh'ol and whose flesh did not see decay.

KJV....... He seeing this before spake of the resurrection of Christ, that his soul was not left in hell, neither his flesh did see corruption.

NIV....... Seeing what was to come, he spoke of the resurrection of the Messiah, that he was not abandoned to the realm of the dead, nor did his body see decay.

5 (c-1) Acts 10: 40

NASB... God raised Him up on the third day and granted that He become visible.

AMP.... God raised Him [to life] on the third day and caused Him to be plainly seen.

CJB....... but God raised him up on the third day and let him be seen,

KJV....... Him God raised up the third day, and shewed him openly;

NIV....... but God raised him from the dead on the third day and caused him to be seen.

5 (c-2) Jn 2: 19

NASB... Jesus answered them, "Destroy this temple, and in three days I will raise it up."

AMP.... Jesus answered them, "Destroy this temple, and in three days I will raise it up."

CJB....... Yeshua answered them, "Destroy this temple, and in three days I will raise it up again."

KJV....... Jesus answered and said unto them, Destroy this temple, and in three days I will raise it up.

NIV...... Jesus answered them, "Destroy this temple, and I will raise it again in three days."

5 (c-3) 1 Cor 15: 4

NASB... and that He was buried, and that He was raised on the third day according to the Scriptures.

AMP.... and that He was buried, and that He was [bodily] raised on the third day according to [that which] the Scriptures [foretold].

CJB....... and he was buried; and he was raised on the third day, in accordance with what the Tanakh says;

KJV....... And that he was buried, and that he rose again the third day according to the scriptures:

NIV....... that he was buried, that he was raised on the third day according to the Scriptures,

5 (d-1) Jn 14:26

NASB... But the Advocate, the Holy Spirit, whom the Father will send in my name, will teach you all things and will remind you of everything I have said to you.

AMP.... But the Helper (Comforter, Advocate, Intercessor - Counselor, Strengthener, Standby), the Holy Spirit, whom the Father will send in My name [in My place, to represent Me and act on My behalf], He will teach you all things. And He will help you remember everything that I have told you.

CJB....... But the Counselor, the Ruach HaKodesh, whom the Father will send in my name, will teach you everything; that is, he will remind you of everything I have said to you.

KJV....... But the Comforter, which is the Holy Ghost, whom the Father will send in my name, he shall teach you all things, and bring all things to your remembrance, whatsoever I have said unto you.

NIV....... But the Advocate, the Holy Spirit, whom the Father will send in my name, will teach you all things and will remind you of everything I have said to you.

5 (d-2) Eph 4:8-13

NASB... Therefore it says, "When He ascended on high, He led captive a host of captives, and He gave gifts to men." (Now this expression, "He ascended," what does it mean except that He also had descended into the lower parts of the earth? He who descended is Himself also He who ascended far above all the heavens, so that He might fill all things.) And He gave some as apostles, and some as prophets, and some as evangelists, and some as pastors and teachers, for the equipping of the saints for the work of service, to the building up of the body of Christ; until we all attain to the unity of the faith, and of the knowledge of the Son of God, to a mature man, to the measure of the stature which belongs to the fullness of Christ.

AMP.... Therefore it says, "When He ascended on high, He led captivity captive, and He bestowed gifts on men." (Now this expression, "He ascended," what does it mean except that He also had previously descended [from the heights of heaven] into the lower parts of the earth? He who descended is the very same as He who also has ascended high above all the heavens, that He [His presence} might fill all things [that is, the whole universe]). And [His gifts to the church were varied and] He Himself appointed some as apostles [special messengers, representatives], some as prophets [who speak a new message from God to the people], some as evangelists [who spread the good news of salvation]. and some as pastors and teachers [to shepherd and guide and instruct], [and He did this] to fully equip and perfect the saints (God's people) for works of service, to build up the body of Christ [the church]; until we all reach oneness in the faith and in the knowledge of the Son of God, [growing spiritually] to become a mature believer, reaching to the measure of the fullness of Christ [manifesting His spiritual completeness and exercising our spiritual gifts, in unity]

CJB.... This is why it says, "After he went up into the heights, he led captivity captive and he gave gifts to mankind." Now this phrase, "he went up." what can it mean if not that he first went down into the lower parts, that is, the earth? The one who went down is himself the one who also went up, far above all of heaven, in order to fill all things. Furthermore, he gave some people as emissaries, some as prophets, some as proclaimers of the Good News, and some as shepherds and teachers. Their task is to equip God's people for the work of service that builds the body of the Messiah, until we all arrive at the unity implied by trusting and knowing the Son of God, at full manhood, at the standard of maturity set by the Messiah's perfection.

KJV.... Wherefore he saith, When he ascended up on high, he led captivity captive, and gave gifts unto men. (Now that he ascended, what is it be that he also descended first into the lower parts of the earth? He that descended is the same also that ascended up far above all heavens, that he might fill all things.) And he gave some, apostles; and some, prophets; and some, evangelists; and some, pastors and teachers; for the perfecting of the saints, for the work of the ministry, for the edifying of the body of Christ: Till we all come in the unity of the faith, and of the knowledge of the Son of God, unto a perfect man, unto the measure of the stature of the fulness of Christ:

NIV....... This is why it says: "When he ascended on high, he took many captives and gave gifts to his people." (What does "he ascended" mean except that he also descended to the lower, earthly regions? He who descended is the very one who ascended higher than all the heavens, in order to fill the whole universe.) So Christ himself gave the apostles, the prophets, the evangelists, the pastors and teachers, to equip his people for works of service, so that the body of Christ may be built up until we all reach unity in the faith and in the knowledge of the Son of God and become mature, attaining to the whole measure of the fullness of Christ.

5 (d-3) Ro 12:6-8

NASB...Since we have gifts that differ according to the grace given to us, each of us is to exercise them accordingly: if prophecy, according to the proportion of his faith; if service, in his serving; or he who teaches, in his teaching; or he who exhorts, in his exhortation; he who gives, with liberality; he who leads, with diligence; he who shows mercy, with cheerfulness.

AMP....Since we have gifts that differ according to the grace given to us, each of us is to use them accordingly: if [someone has the gift of] prophecy, [let him speak a new message from God to His people] in proportion to the faith possessed; if service, in the act of serving; or he who teaches, in the act of teaching; or he who encourages, in the act of encouragement; he who gives, with generosity; he who leads, with diligence; he who show mercy [in caring for others], with cheerfulness.

CJB....... But we have gifts that differ and which are meant to be used according to the grace that has been given to us. If your gift is prophecy, use it to the extent of your trust; if it is serving, use it to serve; if you are a teacher, use your gift in teaching; if you are a counselor, use your gift to comfort and exhort; if you are someone who gives, do it simply and generously, of you are in a position of leadership, lead with diligence and zeal; if you are one who does acts of mercy, do them cheerfully.

KJV....... Having then gifts differing according to the grace that is given to us, whether prophecy, let us prophesy according to the proportion of faith; or ministry, let us wait on our ministering: or he that teacheth, on teaching; or he that exhorteth, on exhortation: he that giveth, let him do it with simplicity; he that ruleth, with diligence; he that sheweth mercy, with cheerfulness.

NIV....... We have different gifts, according to the grace given to each of us. If your gift is prophesying, then prophesy in accordance with your faith; if it is serving, then serve; if it is teaching, then teach; if it is to encourage, then give encouragement; if it is giving, then give generously; if it is to lead, do it diligently; if it is to show mercy, do it cheerfully.

5 (d-4) 1 Cor 12:27-31

NASB...Now you are Christ's body, and individually members of it. And God has appointed in the church, first apostles, second prophets, third teachers, then miracles, then gifts of healings, helps, administrations, various kinds of tongues; All are not apostles, are they? All are not prophets, are they? All are not teachers, are they? All are not workers of miracles, are they? All do not have gifts of healings, do they? All do not speak with tongues, do they? All do not interpret, do they? But earnestly desire the greater gifts. And I show you a still more excellent way.

AMP....Now you [collectively] are Christ's body, and individually [you are] members of it [each with his own special purpose and function]. So God has appointed and placed in the church [for His own use]: first apostles [chosen by Christ], second prophets [those who foretell the future, those who speak a new message from God to the people], third teachers, then those who work miracles, then those with the gifts of healings, the helpers, the administrators, and speakers in various kinds of [unknown] tongues. Are all apostles? Are all prophets? Are all teachers? Are all workers of miracles? Do all have gifts of healing? Do all speak with tongues? Do all interpret? But earnestly desire and strive for the greater gifts [if acquiring them is going to be your goal]. And yet I will show you a still more excellent way [one of the choicest graces and the highest of them all: unselfish love].

CJB....... Now you together constitute the body of the Messiah, and individually you are parts of it. And God has placed in the Messianic Community first, emissaries; second, prophets; third, teachers; then those who work miracles; then those with gifts of healing; those with ability to help; those skilled in administration; and those who speak in various tongues. Not all are emissaries, are they? Not all are prophets, are they? or teachers? or miracle-workers? Not all have gifts of healing, not all speak in tongues, not all interpret, do they? Eagerly seek the better gifts. But now I will show you the best way of all.

KJV....... Now ye are the body of Christ, and members in particular. And God hath set some in the church, first apostles, secondarily prophets, thirdly teachers, after that miracles, then gifts of healings, helps, governments, diversities of tongues. Are all apostles? are all prophets? are all teachers? are all workers of miracles? Have all the gifts of healing? do all speak with tongues? do all interpret? But covet earnestly the best gifts: and yet shew I unto you a more excellent way.

NIV....... Now you are the body of Christ, and each one of you is a part of it. And God has placed in the church first of all apostles, second prophets, third teachers, then miracles, then gifts of healing, of helping, of guidance, and of different kinds of tongues. Are all apostles? Are all prophets? Are all teachers? Do all work miracles? Do all have gifts of healing? Do all speak in tongues? Do all interpret? Now eagerly desire the greater gifts. And yet I will show you the most excellent way.

5 (d-5) Acts 2:38-39

NASB... Peter said to them, "Repent, and each of you be baptized in the name of Jesus Christ for the forgiveness of your sins; and you will receive the gift of the Holy Spirit. For the promise is for you and your children and for all who are far off, as many as the Lord our God will call to Himself."

AMP.... And Peter said to them, "Repent [change your old way of thinking, turn from your sinful ways, accept and follow Jesus as the Messiah] and be baptized, each of you, in the name of Jesus Christ because of the forgiveness of your sins; and you will receive the gift of the Holy Spirit. For the promise [of the Holy Spirit] is for you and your children and for all who are far away [including the Gentiles], as many as the Lord our God calls to Himself."

CJB....... Kefa answered them, "Turn from sin, return to God, and each of you be immersed on the authority of Yeshua the Messiah into forgiveness of your sins, and you will receive the gift of the Ruach HaKodesh! For the promise is for you, for your children, and for those far away -- as many as ADONAI our God may call!"

KJV....... Then Peter said unto them, Repent, and be baptized every one of you in the name of Jesus Christ for the remission of sins, and ye shall receive the gift of the Holy Ghost. For the promise is unto you, and to your children, and to all that are afar off, even as many as the Lord our God shall call.

NIV....... Peter replied, "Repent and be baptized, every one of you, in the name of Jesus Christ for the forgiveness of your sins. And you will receive the gift of the Holy Spirit. The promise is for you and your children and for all who are far off -- for all whom the Lord our God will call."

5 (e) Acts 1 : 3

NASB... To these He also presented Himself alive after His suffering, by many convincing proofs, appearing to them over a period of forty days and speaking of the things concerning the kingdom of God.

AMP.... To these [men] He also showed Himself alive after His suffering [in Gethsemane and on the cross], by [a series of] many infallible proofs and unquestionable demonstrations, appearing to them over a period of forty days and talking to them about the things concerning the kingdom of God.

CJB....... After his death he showed himself to them and gave many convincing proofs that he was alive. During a period of forty days they saw him, and he spoke with them about the Kingdom of God.

KJV....... To whom also he shewed himself alive after his passion by many infallible proofs, being seen of them forty days, and speaking of the things pertaining to the kingdom of God:

NIV .... After his suffering, he presented himself to them and gave many convincing proofs that he was alive. He appeared to them over a period of forty days and spoke about the kingdom of God.

5 (f) I Cor 15: 6

NASB... After that He appeared to more than five hundred brethren at one time, most of whom remain until now, but some have fallen asleep;

AMP.... After that He appeared to more than five hundred brothers and sisters at one time, the majority of whom are still alive, but some have fallen asleep [in death].

CJB....... and afterwards he was seen by more than five hundred brothers at one time, the majority of whom are still alive, though some have died.

KJV....... After that, he was seen of above five hundred brethren at once; of whom the greater part remain unto this present, but some are fallen asleep.

NIV....... After that, he appeared to more than five hundred of the brothers and sisters at the same time, most of whom are still living, though some have fallen asleep.

5 (g-1) Mark 16: 19

NASB... So then, when the Lord Jesus had spoken to them, He was received up into heaven and sat down at the right hand of God.

AMP.... So then, when the Lord Jesus had spoken to them, He was taken up into heaven and sat down at the right hand of God.

CJB....... So then, after he had spoken to them, the Lord Yeshua was taken up into heaven and sat at the right hand of God.

KJV....... So then after the Lord had spoken unto them, he was received up into heaven, and sat on the right hand of God.

NIV....... After the Lord Jesus had spoken to them, he was taken up into heaven and he sat at the right hand of God.

5 (g-2) Luke 24: 50 - 51

NASB... And He led them out as far as Bethany, and He lifted up His hands and blessed them. While He was blessing them, He parted from them and was carried up into heaven.

AMP... Then He led them out as far as Bethany, and lifted up His hands and blessed them. While He was blessing them, He left them and was taken up into heaven.

CJB....... He led them out toward Beit-Anyah; then, raising his hands, he said a b'rakhah over them; and as he was blessing them, he withdrew from them and was carried up into heaven.

KJV....... And he led them out as far as to Bethany, and he lifted up his hands, and blessed them. And it came to pass, while he blessed them, he was parted from them, and carried up into heaven.

NIV....... When he had led them out to the vicinity of Bethany, he lifted up his hands and blessed them. While he was blessing them, he left them and was taken up into heaven.

5 (h-1) Luke 24: 49

NASB... And behold, I am sending forth the promise of My Father upon you; but you are to stay in the city until you are clothed with power from on high.

AMP.... Listen carefully: I am sending the Promise of My Father [the Holy Spirit] upon you; but you are to remain in the city [of Jerusalem] until you are clothed (fully equipped) with power from on high.

CJB....... Now I am sending forth upon you what my Father promised, so stay here in the city until you have been equipped with power from above.

KJV....... And, behold, I send the promise of my Father upon you: but tarry ye in the city of Jerusalem, until ye be endued with power from on high.

NIV....... I am going to send you what my Father has promised; but stay in the city until you have been clothed with power from on high.

5 (h-2) 1Cor 12: 3

NASB... Therefore I make known to you that no one speaking by the Spirit of God says, "Jesus is accursed"; and no one can say, "Jesus is Lord," except by the Holy Spirit.

AMP.... Therefore I want you to know that no one speaking by the [power and influence of the] Spirit of God can say, "Jesus be cursed," and no one can say, "Jesus is [my] Lord," except by [the power and influence of] the Holy Spirit.

CJB....... Therefore, I want to make it clear to you that no one speaking by the Spirit of God ever says, "Yeshua is cursed!" and no one can say, "Yeshua is Lord," except by the Ruach HaKodesh.

KJV....... Therefore I give you to understand, that no man speaking by the Spirit of God calleth Jesus accursed: and that no man can say that Jesus is the Lord, but by the Holy Ghost.

NIV.......Therefore I want you to know that no one who is speaking by the Spirit of God says, "Jesus be cursed," and no one can say, "Jesus is Lord," except by the Holy Spirit.

5 (h-3) Acts 2: 38-39

NASB... Peter said to them, "Repent, and each of you be baptized in the name of Jesus Christ for the forgiveness of your sins; and you will receive the gift of the Holy Spirit. For the promise is for you and your children and for all who are far off, as many as the Lord our God will call to Himself.

AMP.... And Peter said to them, "Repent [change your old way of thinking, turn from your sinful ways, accept and follow Jesus as the Messiah] and be baptized, each of you, in the name of Jesus Christ because of the forgiveness of your sins; and you will receive the gift of the Holy Spirit. For the promise [of the Holy Spirit] is for you and your children and for all who are far away [including the Gentiles], as many as the Lord our God calls to Himself.

CJB....... Kefa answered them, "Turn from sin, return to God, and each of you be immersed on the authority of Yeshua the Messiah into forgiveness of your sins, and you will receive the gift of the Ruach HaKodesh! For the promise is for you, for your children, and for those far away -- as many as Adonai our God may call!"

KJV....... Then Peter said unto them, Repent, and be baptized every one of you in the name of Jesus Christ for the remission of sins, and ye shall receive the gift of the Holy Ghost. For the promise is unto you, and to your children, and to all that are afar off, even as many as the Lord our God shall call.

NIV....... Peter replied, "Repent and be baptized, every one of you, in the name of Jesus Christ for the forgiveness of your sins. And you will receive the gift of the Holy Spirit. The promise is for you and your children and for all who are far off -- for all whom the Lord our God will call."

6 (a-1) Rev 1 :8

NASB... "I am the Alpha and the Omega," says the Lord God, "who is and who was and who is to come, the Almighty."

AMP.... "I am the Alpha and the Omega [the beginning and the End]," says the Lord God, "Who is [existing forever] and Who was [continually existing in the past] and Who is to come, the Almighty [the Omnipotent, the Ruler of all]."

CJB....... "I am the 'A' and the 'Z,'" says Adonai, God of heaven's armies, the One who is, who was and who is coming.

KJV....... I am Alpha and Omega, the beginning and the ending, saith the Lord, which is, and which was, and which is to come, the Almighty.

NIV....... "I am the Alpha and the Omega." says the Lord God, "who is, and who was, and who is to come, the Almighty."

6 (a-2) Rev 22: 13

NASB... I am the Alpha and the Omega, the first and the last, the beginning and the end."

AMP.... I am the Alpha and the Omega, the First and the Last, the Beginning and the End [the Eternal One]."

CJB....... "I am the 'A' and the 'Z,' the First and the Last, the Beginning and the End."

KJV....... I am Alpha and Omega, the beginning and the end, the first and the last.

NIV....... I am the Alpha and the Omega, the First and the Last, the Beginning and the End.

6 (a-3) Rev 21: 6

NASB... Then He said to me, "It is done. I am the Alpha and the Omega, the beginning and the end. I will give to the one who thirsts from the spring of the water of life without cost.

AMP.... And He said to me, "It is done. I am the Alpha and the Omega, the Beginning and the End. To the one who thirsts I will give [water] from the fountain of the water of life without cost.

CJB....... And he said to me, "It is done! I am the 'A' and the 'Z,' the Beginning and the End. To anyone who is thirsty I myself will give water free of charge from the Fountain of Life.

KJV....... And he said unto me, It is done. I am Alpha and Omega, the beginning and the end. I will give unto him that is athirst of the fountain of the water of life freely.

NIV....... He said to me: "It is done. I Am the Alpha and the Omega, the Beginning and the End. To the thirsty I will give water without cost from the spring of the water of life.

6 (b-1) 1 Tim 6: 14 - 16

NASB... that you keep the commandment without stain or reproach until the appearing of our Lord Jesus Christ, which He will bring about at the proper time - He who is the blessed and only Sovereign, the King of kings and Lord of Lords, who alone possesses immortality and dwells in unapproachable light, whom no man has seen or can see. To Him be honor and eternal dominion! Amen.

AMP.... to keep all His precepts without stain or reproach until the appearing of our Lord Jesus Christ, which He will bring about in His own time -- He who is the blessed and only Sovereign [the absolute Ruler], the King of those who reign as kings and Lord of those who rule as Lords, He alone possesses immortality [absolute exemption from death] and lives in unapproachable light, whom no man has ever seen or can see. To Him be honor and eternal power and dominion! Amen.

CJB....... to obey your commission spotlessly and irreproachably until our Lord Yeshua the Messiah appears. His appearing will be brought about in its own time by the blessed and sole Sovereign, who is King of kings and Lord of Lords, who alone is immortal, who dwells in Unapproachable light that no human being has ever seen or can see -- to him be honor and eternal power. Amen.

KJV....... That thou keep this commandment without spot, unrebukable until the appearing of our Lord Jesus Christ: Which in his times he shall shew, who is the blessed and only Potentate, the King of kings, and Lord of Lords; Who only hath immortality, dwelling in the light which no man can approach unto; whom no man hath seen, nor can see: to whom be honor and power everlasting. Amen.

NIV....... to keep this command without spot or blame until the appearing of our Lord Jesus Christ, which God will bring about in his own time-- God, the blessed and only Ruler, the King of kings and Lord of Lords, who alone is immortal and who lives in unapproachable light, whom no one has seen or can see. To him be honor and might forever. Amen.

6 (b-2) Rev 17: 14

NASB... These will wage war against the Lamb, and the Lamb will overcome them, because He is Lord of lords and King of kings, and those who are with him are the called and chosen and faithful."

AMP.... They will wage war against the Lamb (Christ), and the Lamb will triumph and conquer them, because He is Lord of lords and King of kings, and those who are with Him and on His side are the called and chosen (elect) and faithful."

CJB....... They will go to war against the Lamb, but the Lamb will defeat them, because he is Lord of lords and King of kings, and those who are called, chosen and faithful will overcome along with him."

KJV....... These shall make war with the Lamb, and the Lamb shall overcome them: for he is Lord of lords, and King of kings: and they that are with him are called, and chosen, and faithful.

NIV....... They will wage war against the Lamb, but the Lamb will triumph over them because he is Lord of lords and King of kings -- and with him will be his called, chosen and faithful followers."

6 (c) Is 9: 6

NASB... For a child will be born to us, a son will be given to us; And the government will rest on His shoulders; And His name will be called Wonderful Counselor, Mighty God, Eternal Father, Prince of Peace.

AMP.... For to us a Child shall be born, to us a Son shall be given; And the government shall be upon His shoulder, And His name shall be called Wonderful Counselor, Mighty God, Everlasting Father, Prince of Peace.

CJB....... (vs.8) For a child is born to us, a son is given to us; dominion will rest on his shoulders, and he will be given the name Pele-Yo'etz Gibbor Avi-'Ad Sar-Shalom [Wonder of a Counselor, Mighty God, Father of Eternity, Prince of Peace]

KJV....... For unto us a child is born, unto us a son is given: and the government shall be upon his shoulder: and his name shall be called Wonderful, Counselor, The mighty God, The everlasting Father, The Prince of Peace.

NIV....... For to us a child is born, to us a son is given, and the government will be on his shoulders. And he will be called Wonderful Counselor, Mighty God, Everlasting Father, Prince of Peace.

6 (d) Jn 8: 58

NASB... Jesus said to them, "Truly, truly, I say to you, before Abraham was born, I am"

AMP.... Jesus replied, "I assure you and most solemnly say to you, before Abraham was born, I AM."

CJB....... Yeshua said to them, "Yes, indeed! Before Avraham came into being, I AM!"

KJV....... Jesus said unto them, Verily, verily, I say unto you, Before Abraham was, I am.

NIV....... "Very truly I tell you," Jesus answered, "before Abraham was born, I am!"

6 (e) Rev 22: 16

NASB... "I, Jesus, have sent My angel to testify to you these things for the churches. I am the root and the descendant of David, the bright morning star."

AMP.... "I, Jesus, have sent My angel to testify to you and to give you assurance of these things for the churches. I am the Root (the Source, the Life) and the Offspring of David, the radiant and bright Morning Star."

CJB....... "I, Yeshua, have sent my angel to give you this testimony for the Messianic communities. I am the Root and Offspring of David, the bright Morning Star.

KJV....... I Jesus have sent mine angel to testify unto you these things in the churches. I am the root and the offspring of David, and the bright and morning star.

NIV....... "I, Jesus, have sent my angel to give you this testimony for the churches. I am the Root and the Offspring of David, and the bright Morning Star."

6 (f-1) Rev 5: 5

NASB... and one of the elders said to me, "Stop weeping; behold, the Lion that is from the tribe of Judah, the Root of David, has overcome so as to open the book and its seven seals."

AMP.... Then one of the [twenty-four] elders said to me, "Stop weeping! Look closely, the Lion of the tribe of Judah, the Root of David, has overcome and conquered! He can open the scroll and [break] its seven seals."

CJB....... One of the elders said to me, "Don't cry. Look, the Lion of the tribe of Y'hudah, the Root of David, has won the right to open the scroll and its seven seals."

KJV....... And one of the elders saith unto me, Weep not: Behold, the Lion of the tribe of Judah, the Root of David, hath prevailed to open the book, and to loose the seven seals thereof.

NIV....... Then one of the elders said to me, "Do not weep! See, the Lion of the tribe of Judah, the Root of David, has triumphed. He is able to open the scroll and its seven seals."

6 (g) Jn 1: 29

NASB... The next day he saw Jesus coming to him and said, "Behold, the Lamb of God who takes away the sin of the world!

AMP.... The next day he saw Jesus coming to him and said, "Look! The Lamb of God who takes away the sin of the world!

CJB....... The next day Yochanan saw Yeshua coming toward him and said, "Look! God's lamb! The one who is taking away the sin of the world!

KJV....... The next day John seeth Jesus coming unto him, and saith, Behold the Lamb of God, which taketh away the sin of the world.

NIV....... The next day John saw Jesus coming toward him and said, "Look, the Lamb of God, who takes away the sin of the world!

6 (h-1) Ro 5: 9 - 11

NASB... Much more then, having now been justified by His blood, we shall be saved from the wrath of God through Him. For if while we were enemies we were reconciled to God through the death of His Son, much more, having been reconciled, we shall be saved by His life. And not only this, But we also exult in God through our Lord Jesus Christ. through whom we have now received the reconciliation.

AMP.... Therefore, since we have now been justified [declared free of the guilt of sin] by His blood, [how much more certain is it that] we will be saved from the wrath of God through Him. For if while we were enemies we were reconciled to God through the death of His Son, it is much more certain, having been reconciled, that we will be saved [from the consequences of sin] by His life [that is, we will be saved because Christ lives today]. Not only that, but we also rejoice in God [rejoicing in His love and perfection] through our Lord Jesus Christ, through whom we have now received and enjoy our reconciliation [with God].

CJB....... Therefore, since we have now come to be considered righteous by means of his bloody sacrificial death, how much more will we be delivered through him from the anger of God's judgment! For if we were reconciled with God through his Son's death when we were enemies, how much more will we be delivered by his life, now that we are reconciled! And not only will we be delivered in the future, but we are boasting about God right now, because he has acted through our Lord Yeshua the Messiah, through whom we have already received that reconciliation.

KJV....... Much more then, being now justified by his blood, we shall be saved from wrath through him. For if, when we were enemies, we were reconciled to God by the death of his Son, much more, being reconciled, we shall be saved by his life. And not only so, but we also joy in God through our Lord Jesus Christ, by whom we have now received the atonement.

NIV....... Since we have now been justified by his blood, how much more shall we be saved from God's wrath through him! For if, while we were God's enemies, we were reconciled to him through the death of his Son, how much more, having been reconciled, shall we be saved through his life! Not only is this so, but we also boast in God through our Lord Jesus Christ, through whom we have now received reconciliation.

6 (h-2) Ro 5: 15

NASB... But the free gift is not like the transgression. For if by the transgression of the one the many died, much more did the grace of God and the gift by the grace of the one Man, Jesus Christ, abound to the many.

AMP.... But the free gift [of God] is not like the trespass [because the gift of grace overwhelms the fall of man]. For if many died by one man's trespass [Adam's sin], much more [abundantly] did God's grace and the gift [that comes] by the grace of the one Man, Jesus Christ, overflow to [benefit] the many.

CJB....... But the free gift is not like the offence. For if, because of one man's offence, many died, then how much more has God's grace, that is, the gracious gift of one man, Yeshua the Messiah, overflowed to many!

KJV....... But not as the offence, so also is the free gift. For if through the offence of one many be dead, much more the grace of God, and the gift by grace, which is by one man, Jesus Christ, hath abounded unto many.

NIV...... But the gift is not like the trespass. For if the many died by the trespass of the one man, how much more did God's grace and the gift that came by the grace of the one man, Jesus Christ, overflow to the many!

6 (h-3) Luke 22: 69 - 70

NASB... But from now on the son of man will be seated at the right hand of the power of God." And they all said, "Are Thou the Son of God, then?" And He said to them, "Yes, I am."

AMP.... But from now on the Son of Man will be seated at the right hand of the power of God." And they all said, "Are You the Son of God, then?" He replied, "It is just as you say."

CJV....... But from now on, the Son of Man will be sitting at the right hand of HaG'vurah." They all said, "Does this mean, then, that you are the Son of God?" And he answered them, "You say I am."

KJV....... Hereafter shall the Son of man sit on the right hand of the power of God. Then said they all, Art thou then the Son of God? And he said unto them, Ye say that I am.

NIV....... But from now on, the Son of Man will be seated at the right hand of the mighty God." They all asked, "Are you then the Son of God?" He replied, "You say that I am."

7 (a-1) Rev 1: 17 -18

NASB... When I saw Him, I fell at His feet like a dead man. And He placed His right hand on me, saying, "Do not be afraid; I am the first and the last, and the living One; and I was dead, and behold, I am alive forevermore, and I have the keys of death and of Hades.

AMP.... When I saw Him, I fell at His feet as though dead. And He placed His right hand on me and said, "Do not be afraid; I am the First and the

Last [absolute Deity, the Son of God], and the Ever-living One [living in and beyond all time and space]. I died, but see, I am alive forevermore, and I have the keys of [absolute control and victory over] death and of Hades (the realm of the dead).

CJB....... When I saw him, I fell down at his feet like a dead man. He placed his right hand upon me and said, "Don't be afraid! I am the First and the Last, the Living One. I was dead, but look! -- I am alive forever and ever! And I hold the keys to Death and Sh'ol.

KJV....... And when I saw him, I fell at his feet as dead. And he laid his right hand upon me, saying unto me, Fear not; I am the first and the last: I am he that liveth, and was dead; and, behold, I am alive for evermore, Amen; and have the keys of hell and of death.

NIV....... When I saw him, I fell at his feet as though dead. Then he placed his right hand on me and said: "Do not be afraid. I am the First and the Last. I am the Living One; I was dead, and now look, I am alive for ever and ever! And I hold the keys of death and Hades.

7 (a-2) Jn 11: 25 - 26

NASB... Jesus said to her, "I am the resurrection and the life; he who believes in Me will live even if he dies. and everyone who lives and believes in Me will never die. Do you believe this?"

AMP.... Jesus said to her, "I am the Resurrection and the Life. Whoever believes in (adheres to, trusts in, relies on) Me [as Savior] will live even if he dies; and everyone who lives and believes in Me [as Savior] will never die. Do you believe this?

CJB....... Yeshua said to her, "I AM the Resurrection and the Life! Whoever puts his trust in me will live, even if he dies; and everyone living and trusting in me will never die. Do you believe this?"

KJV........ Jesus said unto her, I am the resurrection, and the life: he that believeth in me, though he were dead, yet shall he live: And whosoever liveth and believeth in me shall never die. Believest thou this?

NIV....... Jesus said to her, "I am the resurrection and the life. The one who believes in me will live, even though they die; and whoever lives by believing in me will never die. Do you believe this?"

8 (Jn 1: 1)

NASB... In the beginning was the Word, and the Word was with God, and the Word was God.

AMP.... In the beginning [before all time] was the Word (Christ), and the Word was God Himself.

CJB....... In the beginning was the Word, and the Word was with God, and the Word was God.

KJV........ In the beginning was the Word, and the Word was with God, and the Word was God.

NIV........ In the beginning was the Word, and the Word was with God, and the Word was God.

The Book: Comments by a non-scholar

Many, if not all, of the scriptures referred to in "Who Is, This, Jesus" are easily understood, clear, and straightforward. However, some doctrines of various denominations or subdivisions of the Church have, over time, drifted from what is actually written. Consequently, when one who is well versed in his or her particular church doctrine reads a verse, they may interpret it through the filter of their accepted doctrine rather than what the scripture actually says. To stray from the accepted interpretation of a scripture by denominational doctrine places the reader in the rather uncomfortable position of fearing rejection by their peers and/or leaders and that fear of rejection can lead to accepting doctrine over scripture. Scripture should trump doctrine until additional scripture clarifies the first scripture to support the doctrine. The gentile mind-set is that since the Jews were given the Law and failed to follow it to God's displeasure, we need a law to follow and be better than they; i.e. "Give me a law that I might make myself to be pleasing to God'" (I did not originate that statement) Consequently, a scripture is all too often taken out of context, exaggerated, and formed into a doctrine of a denomination which identifies "us" as being better than others for "we" are walking closer to God and that doctrine must therefore not be questioned. Quite frankly, that is a dead work and constitutes part of what 1 Cor 3:11-15 refers to as wood hay and straw, "Give me a law that I might make myself to be pleasing unto God."

Clearly, by scriptural reference, Part 1 is referring to Jesus Christ, the Son of God. [Please note that Christ is not Jesus' last name. Written Jesus Christ it is understood to mean Jesus the Christ. Christ means Savior.] One part of this paragraph deserves some clarification. "He learned obedience through His sufferings". When one thinks of the sufferings of Christ, it is natural to picture the crucifixion. Certainly, He was obedient to suffer the crucifixion, but that is not what this scripture refers to. Jesus had to learn something through those sufferings referred to here. He had to live beyond those sufferings to be able to apply what He had learned into His life. He learned that by resisting His natural human nature of self-preservation (or submitting to desires of self-worship) and submitting to the Father's ways (obedience) He was pleasing to the Father and, thereby, won every spiritual battle.

The denying of what the human nature wants is a suffering experience and is worthless unless the self- character is replaced with Godly character. This is our spiritual battle. To fulfill the scripture to put off the old man and putting on the new man in the likeness of Christ is a suffering experience. Jesus fulfilled it because He was God-man. We fulfill it because we become an image of God-man by the Holy Spirit of God dwelling and working within us. The Holy Spirit enables us to make the character change if our self-will allows it to happen. True change is accomplished only by the Holy Spirit's work in us when we willfully submit to Him. We cannot accomplish a change which is pleasing to Him without Him actually doing the work. We can only, through self-will, submit.

His suffering was the crying out of His human desire to manifest the deeds of the flesh rather than do His Father's will in any given situation. The Father's will was and is always to manifest the fruit of the Holy Spirit. For example, Jesus worked as a carpenter. When He hit his hand with a hammer His flesh wanted to scream and utter profanities. His suffering was the rejecting of that desire and manifesting a fruit of the Spirit – perhaps temperance. He certainly regretted the pain, perhaps He screamed, but he did not have an outburst of anger, for such would have been a deed of the flesh, i.e., sin. Though He may have been angry He did not sin, for the Word says, "Be angry and sin not" (Eph 4:26). When He labored to make a piece of furniture only to not have the parts fit properly together, He exhibited patience by His obedience to the Father to start over if necessary and by rejecting His human desire of the flesh to self-justify with excuses. When He was unjustly criticized for a piece of work, He did not exalt His work above that of another but presented His work with humility. You see, in each case of life's circumstances He suffered through the process of denying self-rights (self-worship) and conformed to the will of the Father. This was for Him and is for us a spiritual battle of putting off the old self and putting on the new self as referred to in Eph 4:22-24. In His case, He put on the self of the Father. In our case, it is putting on the new self in the image of Christ. When that is done frequently enough, the old self dies and the suffering is over for that character trait. However, we can always choose to revert back to the old self by choice – bad choice. I'm sure glad Jesus chose never to revert back, for to do so would have been sin.

As believers pursuing to be pleasing to the Father, we cannot put off the old man without submitting to the power of the Holy Spirit to provide a way for us to do so. To try to do His will on our own to make ourselves pleasing to Him will always fail in the long run, because it fosters spiritual arrogance and is a dead work, i.e., wood, hay, and stubble of 1 Cor 3:9-12. (KJV)

So, Jesus suffered the dying of His flesh (self-worship) from His youth throughout His entire life. He had to learn the benefits of obedience to the Father as we are expected to do also, through the process of suffering the death of the flesh. Again, "the flesh" is simply referring to self-worship or putting what we as individuals want above what God wants for us. It is really tied to selfishness and greed; and is usually associated with physical pleasure. Therefore, the reference as "the flesh" or behavior submitted to the flesh rather than behavior that is pleasing to God. We must realize God gave mankind self-will for a reason. He wants us to have fellowship with Him without us losing sight of His position as the Creator. He extends Himself to us through Jesus the Savior and only through Jesus the Savior. Our choosing submission to Him via our self-will does not hinder but rather enhances our own position before all His creation because we have the right to choose to do so or choose not to do so. The Church is elevated to a position, through obedience, to reveal the fulfillment of Ephesians 3: 9-12.

The warfare occurs in the mind. Remember heart, mind, soul, and strength? The Father wants His children to behave in the manner He has described in His Word. The Holy Spirit is joined to your heart (spirit) and presents to the mind the direction He wants the mind to take. The unrenewed portion of your mind wants to please self rather than God. Thus, the warfare takes place. The process of submitting the flesh to the Spirit is the suffering so long as the mind is not completely renewed. As the mind repeatedly submits to the Spirit in that particular character trait, the mind is more and more renewed and the suffering is less and less because the Spirit then rules and the mind is no longer tempted to follow the flesh. That is the process of change the Father wants us to have and the consequence is, concerning that character trait, righteousness, peace, and joy in the Holy Spirit. In other words, you have willingly received the sovereign reign of God in that area of your life. Such is the Kingdom of God, one character trait at a time.

The wisdom of God is unlimited and as He shares His wisdom with us, we get a glimpse of its multifaceted or manifold aspects, all of which overcome evil and all of which more tightly unite the mind with the spirit/Spirit in willful submission to Him. As the mind is submitted to the Holy Spirit, the soul of man reflects this union. In other words, different believers going through the same process each reflect through their individual souls or individualities the character of Christ. One mature Christian will know what another mature Christian will do in a given situation because they will be like minded with renewed minds in the image of Christ. The intensity of the renewal is directly related to strength applied by the Christian directed toward the transition from the old man to the new. "Love the Lord thy God with all your heart, mind, soul, and strength." And, as the process proceeds, the manifold wisdom of God is revealed to the powers and principalities in the heavenly places. Little by little, one step at a time, we reveal His sovereignty to His creation and receive the benefits of righteousness, peace, and joy as we walk out this life which He has given to us. As the transition from old self to new self occurs, we become more and more obedient to His Word without suffering. Thus, we fulfill 1 Jn 5:3. We can be obedient to His Word without it being a burden to do so.

Let's say, for example, that you are a thief. You are a good thief and have never been caught. You come to know the Lord and the Holy Spirit takes residence within you and unites with your spirit. Suddenly you realize you should not steal, because you read in the bible that God does not want you to steal. Your flesh enjoys the "benefits" of your life as a thief and it is so easy for you to do. Your mind really does not want to quit. Yet, within you is now a sense of guilt that was not there before. The Spirit is dealing with you. You know that you know that you know that what you are doing is wrong so you pray God will grant you the strength (remember heart, mind, soul, and STRENGTH) to be obedient to His Word. The warfare begins over your soul (individual personality). You start sharpening your sword (Eph 6:17) by studying His Word. When you are presented with an opportunity to steal (temptation) you draw your sword and strike with scripture that which you have loved in the past but you now know is displeasing to your heavenly Father. Perhaps the pain of self-denial is too great and you succumb. That little thing you stole was really not worth much, so why do you keep thinking about it? OK, so you know you really shouldn't have done that and you'll try not to do it again, you say to yourself. Since you are new at this repentance stuff, you really don't want to admit to God that you sinned. You forget He already knows. Finally, you repent to your Heavenly Father, and promise you will never do that again. So, you go through this process several times until your Heavenly Father decides you need to mature a bit. Thus, His chastisement begins. He gets quiet to you and you probably get out of reading the Word. Now, this story can get pretty ugly, so let's change the process by saying after you repented the first time you studied His Word, sharpened your sword and thickened your shield so when temptation occurred again you blocked it by faith and slashed it to pieces with your knife-edged sword of the Word. You won! You did not steal! It was tough but the victory was yours and you revealed God's character through your behavior. Rest assured, it will happen again, but it will be a shorter fight the next time as the character of Christ is strengthened within you. And you have peace. "There is therefore now no condemnation for them who are in Christ Jesus" (Ro 8:1).

In part 2, Jesus presented a truth that the worldly could not understand. Those ruled by their flesh cannot accept anything that threatens self. To love the Lord your God with all your heart, mind, soul, and strength and to love one's neighbor as one's self requires the willingness to deny self-worship. To get a grasp on Mark 12: 30-31 requires an understanding of what the words love, heart, mind, soul, strength, and neighbor actually mean. Otherwise, it just sounds spiritual and sort of poetic, but its application is generally not expected by the reader.

Concerning love:

The different Greek words for the English word love are good to know, but not necessary for us to understand what the Lord is saying here. This love is all encompassing. It is not dependent on emotion although it can include emotion. It is the perfect love that casts out all fear (which is an emotion) and is best defined biblically in 1 Jn 5:3. "For this is the love of God, that we keep His commandments; and His commandments are not burdensome" (NASB). It is vital to recognize the last part of this verse, for to keep His commandments in a "must do" attitude is being under the Law. There is no life there. It's like trying to make the old man (self) righteous through good works. Only by relying on God's Holy Spirit dwelling within us can we get past the suffering flesh and put on the new man which is in the likeness of Him. Only then can we come to the point of fulfilling His commandments without being burdened to do so. Also, it is vital to properly understand the scripture you are pursuing to fulfill and what part of your character you should change. As the change is more and more accomplished, the character of Christ within us, our hope for glory from the Father, becomes more and more our norm. We can be confident we are recognized in that character trait by the Father as having the same character trait as Christ Himself because only through the Holy Spirit can that behavior be achieved. Then, when we peacefully manifest the character of Christ by our behavior, we reveal and express the manifold wisdom of God to the powers and principalities in high or heavenly places. We reveal that good overcomes evil, encourage His holy angels, and humiliate the fallen angels before all of God's creation.

We can think of glory as positive recognition. For us to have glory before Almighty God our Creator, is for us to receive positive recognition by Him or for us to be pleasing to Him. He shares His glory with no-one but He Himself becomes our glory (Ps. 3:3). That can only happen when He sees in us a reflection of the character of His beloved Son, Jesus Christ. God has chosen to love all mankind. Without being burdened, He is obedient to His own word in His relationship with all of us and that is done without partiality.

Concerning the heart:

The heart of man is his inner-most being, the life force breathed into mankind by God Himself, the spirit of mankind which hungers for union with its Maker. Man's drive to follow his heart is meant for his good. When one accepts Jesus Christ as his personal Lord and Savior, the Spirit of God takes residence with the heart or spirit of the person. Thus, the drive to follow one's heart is designed to be the drive to follow the Spirit of God, because of the marriage of the two. However, God wants this relationship to be in accord with man's ability to choose. Thus, we must go through the process of change through the sufferings of change previously discussed. When we love God with our hearts, we recognize our life is His with Jesus Christ as our rock to anchor our behavior to His ways. When we accept the Lord as Savior, we experience a heart change by the presence of the Holy Spirit. Character change of the believer evidences the presence of the Holy Spirit of God working actively from within the person. Yet, He has chosen for us all, just as He did for Jesus Christ, to have to choose by ever present self-will to continue to choose His will and His ways over our own. And in doing so we show by our behavior that good triumphs over evil.

Concerning the mind:

2 Tim 1: 7 was written to Timothy (and us) as encouragement that our God has not given to us His Holy Spirit to instill in us spiritual timidity, but rather "power and love and discipline" (NASB). The Amplified Bible says "…power and of love and of sound judgment and personal discipline [abilities that result in a calm, well-balanced mind and self-control]". The Complete Jewish Bible says "…but power, love, and self-discipline. And, the KJV says "… but of power, and of love, and of a sound mind." By comparing these versions, we can see that the mind is related to decision making and judgment. It is the filter between thought and action. The mind is the decision-making part of one's self using memories, ideas, options, and reasonings to balance actions rather than having actions merely responses to emotions. When we love God with our minds, we submit to the Holy Spirit to renew our ways of thinking and reasoning to line up with His ways as revealed in His Word, the Bible.

Concerning soul:

Mankind's souls distinguish each person apart from the other. Related to personality, it is the inner-self revealed through relationships with other people. Where the spirit is necessary for life, the soul distinguishes one life from another. When we love God with our soul, we submit our personalities to become reflections of His ways.

Concerning strength:

Including but not limited to the physical, strength includes determination and focus. Once what is right is determined by the mind through influence of the soul (psyche) and heart (spirit) one's strength (determination) presses mankind into an action. When we love God with our strength, our pursuit is His will replacing our will anywhere our actions would be contrary to His ways.

Love the Lord your God with all your heart, mind, soul, and strength. Such is all dependent on your self-will which God chose for you to have from the beginning. We have the ability to choose. Choose to have your mind stayed on Christ -------------------. Choose to have your personality be evidence of Christ within you -----------------. Choose to focus your determination on fulfilling His word .... Choose to pray, if you haven't before, that Jesus would fill you with His Holy Spirit so as to enable you by your life to evidence His life within you. God is near to us, but He has chosen to give us self-will to legitimize our witness of Him to the powers and principalities in high places (Eph. 3:9-12), as well as to future believers who want to see Christ through us. May we be pleasing to the Father by being reflections of His Son Jesus Christ as He looks at us.

Concerning neighbor:

Certainly, we are to wish no harm on anyone but are to hope for all to come to the Lord. But all people are not our neighbors. Jesus separated the love of self from the love of God. We are to love the Lord our God with all we are. We are not called to love ourselves or other people with such intensity. In Luke 10:25-37 a lawyer, after Jesus identified the second greatest law, asked Him who was his neighbor. Jesus' parable sited a man beaten and left helpless on a road. Three different men at three different times came upon him. The first two chose not to help him but the third showed compassion on the injured man and helped him. Jesus taught that the first two men, by not helping the injured man, were not his neighbors. The third man was the hurt man's neighbor by his actions. By this, the second most important commandment, the hurt man is to love as himself the man who helped him. He is under no obligation to love the other two men as himself. Thus, the one who receives loving kindness from someone is expected by the Lord to extend loving kindness in return, not as required by law but as fulfilled by one's spirit being submitted to the Spirit.

One might ask if a month later the roles were reversed and the man who had been hurt came upon one of those who would not help him in a ditch having been beaten and robbed. We-e-e-e-ll, though not obligated by their previous actions to love those two as himself, he and we are expected by the Lord to be compassionate. Jesus told the lawyer to go and do the same as the Samaritan. What better way to manifest the loving kindness of Christ than to help someone who previously denied help to you?

Part 3 presents the crucifixion as we must realize to grasp the ugliness of our sins before God. If we were the only people to exist, we would have to be the ones to torture and crucify the Lamb of God for us to be saved. There is no distinction between us and His torturers over two thousand years ago. We are each personally responsible for His brutal, barbaric treatment unto His death.

Part 4 tells of the events which immediately followed the death of the Lord Jesus Christ. Please note that He died in darkness (night), just as Jonah was swallowed by the great fish in darkness. On the third period of light (day) following the first night, Jonah was thrown onto dry land. On the third period of light following Jesus' death in darkness, He arose.

Part 5 pertains to what happened from the time Jesus arose until His ascension to the Father. In the verses listed there are some suggestions that Jesus was hard to recognize. But His identity was verified by His actions and behavior. Please note, Jesus' body upon its restoration to life initially must have looked as it did following His crucifixion (Jn 20: 27). Being alive it was undoubtably healing, but He also showed the aftermath of being beaten on His face and head with a ridged stick, slapped repeatedly, and His beard was partially torn out of His face. With His face bruised and swollen He would have been hard to recognize at first. As He taught about His kingdom for forty days, the healing process continued. His voice and mannerisms verified His identity.

After He ascended to the Father the stage was set for the events of Pentecost. It is interesting to note that the word Pentecost is the Greek word referring to the celebration of the day the Jews received the Law at Mt. Sinai. God the Father sent God the Holy Spirit to empower Jesus Christ's disciples to fulfill the Law on the anniversary of His giving the Law to Moses. In Jn 20:21-22 (NASB) the bible reveals when Jesus first appeared to His disciples. After recognizing Him they rejoiced and Jesus said to them "Peace be with you; as the Father has sent Me, I also send you." [Then] He breathed on them and said to them "Receive the Holy Spirit". Here Jesus did a conscious and deliberate act of breathing on each of His disciples present in that room. We don't know how many disciples were there. We do know Thomas was named as not being there and Mary Magdalene was. Whether there were a few or 120 as were at Pentecost, we cannot be sure. But we can be certain Jesus deliberately breathed on each of them and in doing so said to them "Receive the Holy Spirit". Here, the Greek word for breath is the same word for spirit. The disciples received the Holy Spirit at that time, as commanded by the Lord. The promise of receiving the Holy Spirit as security of salvation occurred to His Church at that time. In other words, the Church was born. What He did physically then, He does spiritually since. Salvation occurs when by faith we ask, and the Holy Spirit is at that time given to the believer as the guarantee of that salvation. Yet, they were at that time ordered to wait in Jerusalem (Acts 1:4-5) for what we now call Pentecost. The grand entrance of His bride to the world by God's blessing of power from on high was about to explode before His creation like our fourth of July fireworks. What John the Baptist prophesied about the Messiah (Matt. 3:11) was about to occur.

Part 6 are the metaphors used in the Bible in referring to Jesus Christ.

Part 7 "He says" refers to the timelessness of God. Just as He spoke to John over two thousand years ago, He could say the same today and forever in the future without changing the meaning of who He is.

The last of Part 8 reflects the timelessness of God as in Part 7. From our perspective, Jesus as the Christ was not born in the beginning, but in God's perspective He has always been and will always be.

One Secret Revealed

Have you ever wondered if there is a reason why you exist? Is there something special the Lord designed you to fulfill or accomplish in this life? Well, I am here to say there is a calling for you. There is a task of opportunities for you as an individual which are unique in design to fit you in this life, in your circumstances of life, which only you can accomplish. The basic pattern of success in these tasks is outlined for you as with all other believers, but only you can apply them to your life to accomplish the conversion God wants for you. He promises to provide for you the physical needs you have if you will pursue the spiritual calling He has for you.

God chose to create you to be an instrument for His glory. This one true God has chosen to create mankind; and, for His good pleasure He chose to create YOU and me. Along with creating us, He has chosen to reveal Himself to us in three distinctions. God the Father, God the Son, and God the Holy Spirit. He is still one God but we can better understand Him as three aspects and since He has chosen to do so in this way, who are we to disagree? Bear with me now. Why I am presenting what you already know will soon be evident.

The Father is the authoritarian head. He sets the guidelines He wants us, His adopted children, to follow in order to both please Him and to benefit or prosper via His guidance. A key to this prosperity is for our behavior to be as His role-model for us and Savior for us Jesus Christ. His name is Jesus. His function according to the Father's will is Christ, Savior, Messiah. All three terms mean the same thing, and in this capacity, He serves the Father's will as the Son. So, for eternal salvation our complete trust is in Jesus the Savior. But, what about now? Is salvation only for the future when we leave these bodies of clay?

By reading the Bible and listening to preachers we know we are supposed to be good. But that can be hard to do, and besides, "I'm a believer and I have eternal life and I'm good most of the time. So, what's the big deal? If I sin, I'll be forgiven so I'll do the best I can, trust Jesus to save me, and not worry about the rest." Well, we find that God has more ways to deal with mankind than to send him to hell. It all depends on attitude. If you truly believe what I just wrote is all there is, wait a bit and see if God wants you to do more. You will know, when problems arise and you cannot deal with them. That's called chastisement. Or, if you stiffen your resistance to serve Him who has given you salvation by His personal sacrifice via crucifixion, read Rev.3:15-16, and remember, peace is given through repentance. The Lord chastens his children for our correction out of His love for us (Rev 3:19).I have experienced His chastening and each time it has been painful. But I have seen severe chastisement from the Lord to believers who just would not self-evaluate their behavior. It's not fun and I want no part of it. We can learn by observation without being judgmental for the Lord does the judging and we can learn by observation. The Lord loves His children. His love is pure and without partiality and is clarified in 1 Jn 5:3. He has chosen to obey His own Word.

Now, God has not called all to preach, or evangelize, or pastor, or teach, or anything in the back of your mind that you are afraid to do. But, He has called all of us to have a character change and reveal that in our behavior. He tells us in the Book of James that faith (trust) without works (behavior) is dead. The behavior we are to have is to reveal the character of Christ within us. Christ in us, the hope of glory. We can only imitate His character temporarily by acting (hypocrisy) unless we have gone through the process of putting off the old man and putting on the new man in the likeness of Christ. He really does want us to live happy, fulfilled lives, blessed at every turn in this life, but He has established cause/effect spiritual laws which He will not change. One of those is the calling of His Church to reveal His manifold or multifaceted wisdom by being transformed from our former self, regardless of how good or bad we were, by trusting Him (faith) to help us make that change, i.e., the putting on of the character of Christ. I am not talking about salvation from Hell here. Only God knows some things including who His children are. You should know as well about yourself and if you don't you should ask Him to reveal your own salvation to you. He opens the door of salvation for our old man but wants our new man to dwell with Him and be blessed beyond measure in communion with Him as we live the lives we now have. I am not referring to the "name it and claim it" financial prosperity messages, but rather to the spiritual life changes which enable us to have the ability to manifest the amazing multifaceted wisdom of God our Creator not just to ourselves and those people around us but to the powers and principalities in high places of spiritual authority which for now are a little more powerful than are we. (Eph 3:9-12 and Ps 8:5) Why has He done that? I suspect for His good pleasure.

You will reap what you sow. When it comes to reaping what is sown, most sermons I have heard lead up to an increase in giving money to the church. That is not what I am talking about. I want you to see how to win spiritual battles which occur almost daily. As you do, you will find your priorities will change. You will find that our Father really does know our needs before we do and by seeking first His Kingdom, He will provide for your physical needs much better than you have been able to do yourself. His Kingdom simply refers to HIS sovereignty through your submission. God is going to be sovereign regardless. He is sovereign in heaven, on earth, in hell, and throughout the entire universe both physical and spiritual. He is ….. period. Think of entering into His Kingdom as accepting what He has provided for us, to have a personal relationship with Him which can only come through the way He has provided, which is through His Son, Jesus Christ. But, not only this but committing our lives to this relationship to find righteousness, peace, and joy in the Holy Spirit. We work, but not for salvation from hell. Our work is the putting on of the new man (Eph 4:24).But, even though that is labor intense, we accomplish it not by our own strength or determination but by using our self-will to yield to Him. In Phil3, Paul wrote of attaining to the resurrection from the dead. Attain means to obtain with effort. We do not obtain with effort our salvation. It is a free gift from God through faith (trust). Paul's writing of knowing Him and the power of His resurrection and the fellowship of His sufferings and being conformed to His death, all refer to the exchanging of carnal self for the character of Christ to experience Christ in us, our hope of glory, real and active in this life we live. It sounds like a great trade to me. Instead of worrying and struggling and envying and being guilt-ridden, we can walk in peace beyond understanding and have great joy by letting the Holy Spirit guide us into a life of righteousness and walk out each day winning every conflict which will challenge that. You see, that's really what our existence is all about. We, the Church as individuals, are to demonstrate before all creation that Jesus Christ is Lord to the glory of God the Father through submission to His Holy Spirit by trust. We, through self-will can choose to allow Christ to reign as Lord of our lives on a daily basis.

"I have come to give you life, and life more abundantly" (Jn 10:19). Prior to salvation, we were dead in our trespasses and sins. Jesus gives us life when we were born again by His Holy Spirit. The life more abundantly comes as we convert from our old ways, referred to as the flesh, to our new ways which are His ways which are spiritual. Because the Father has set spiritual laws which affect the physical and because He wants us to reveal His wisdom in battle before all His creation, He has established a cause/effect system which He has chosen to be fact. He will not change it for you, and He will not change it for me. Jesus won every spiritual conflict, pleasing the Father and encouraging the holy angels while humiliating the fallen angels before all creation. He wants us to do the same, being reflections of Jesus. The new man which we actively put on is in the likeness of Christ; the character of Christ replacing our old carnal thinking and thereby changing our behavior.

The foundation of the Church is Jesus Christ (1 Cor 3:11). Yet, Eph 2:20 reads Jesus Christ as being the chief cornerstone and refers to the Church as being built upon the foundation of the apostles and prophets. The Church being built upon the foundation of the apostles and prophets does not mean the foundation is comprised of apostles and prophets, but rather the foundation owned by or belonging to or laid by the apostles and prophets. The entire foundation of the church is Jesus. The chief cornerstone is Jesus the Christ or Savior. The rest of the foundation is the character of Jesus or, if you will, the character of God. That was, some would say "is", the function of the apostles and prophets. It is to reveal to the Church the character of God as a guideline of life, thus establishing and stabilizing the Church. We, as individuals of the Church, are to build upon this foundation with behavior which matches the individual character traits of God which make up this foundation. We put a block of love upon the foundation stone of love, a block of faith upon the foundation stone of faith, a block of gentleness on a stone of gentleness and so on throughout our lives. If we do what looks like a generous deed but our motive is self-recognition, or some other deed of the flesh, we have just put a block of hay on a selflessness stone of the foundation. When tried by fire before the Lord it will be burned up and we will suffer loss. If the deed reflects a true character trait of Christ it will be represented by a precious stone laid upon that character trait foundation block of Jesus. The deeds, or work, or behavior done by a believer which reflect a character trait of God functioning within the believer are the gems which survive the test of fire and are worthy of representing rewards to the believer. A non-believer who does something good with a Christ-like motive is prohibited from building on the foundation because one must pass first over the chief cornerstone which is Jesus the Savior, thus no one can achieve salvation by works alone. There is no access to the rest of the Church's foundation on which to build. All of this may be earthly metaphorical or heavenly reality. Regardless, they are spiritually accurate. Thank God, our salvation is not the question here (1 Cor 3:15). The question is how many precious stones of Jesus' character will glow through the testing by fire at judgement, and how well can we manifest the manifold wisdom of God to the powers and principalities in high places while we walk this earth as children of the Most-High God.

I don't want to get wrapped up in denominational church doctrine here, but I do believe this warrants stating. In what we call the great commission, Jesus commanded His apostles to go into all the world preaching salvation through Him and baptizing in the name of the Father, the Son, and the Holy Spirit. He commanded them to wait for what we call Pentecost to receive the power to do that. For the rest of their lives, they went into all the world preaching salvation through Him and baptizing in the name of Jesus. Think about it.

Situation Application

As believers, we are subject to different rules of expectations than are non-believers. We are told in the Bible to put off the old man and put on the new man in the likeness of Christ (Eph4:22-24). How?

When we were created, God gave us the right to self-will. In other words, we have the God-given right to choose to do something His way or not His way. Since He is never wrong, it's really not very efficient to not do something His way because the other way fails and we are presented with the issue again, and again, and again until we do it His way and the spiritual conflict is resolved. If we never learn, it is never resolved. Like it or not, although our physical well-being is very important to our Heavenly Father, our spiritual well-being is of greater importance to Him. Once our decisions are to promote our spiritual well-being through obedience to His ways following submission to His truths, He provides for those physical needs we have been warring and struggling to obtain. That is another way of saying seek first His kingdom then all your needs will be met. It's simply a matter of priorities. If your priorities are wrong, you are on your own. If they are right, He will provide for you sufficiently. If you fear He will not give you as much as you want, the best thing for you to do is repent. Along with that, understand you cannot bribe or bargain with your Creator. I have heard it said and taught "you cannot out give God". Well, you most assuredly can if you are trying to force Him to give you something. Those who teach such are the recipients of your giving. They are probably teaching the tithe goes to the Levites, guess who the Levites are. There is ample support in the New Testament for giving and sometimes giving sacrificially, but there is no support for giving a set percentage, by law. The only guidance we have is that the Lord loves a cheerful giver. So, give what makes you happy. If a set percentage does so, give a set percentage, but don't think you can purchase God's blessing on your remaining if you give to Him a set amount. The way to receive the blessings of God is to seek first His Kingdom of righteousness, peace, and joy in the Holy Spirit by welcoming His sovereignty in your every-day life. He is your Father and He wants good things for you first spiritually, then physically.

Prior to accepting Jesus Christ as your Lord and Savior your battles were for preservation of self. With the Holy Spirit dwelling within you as a believer, your battles should be for the conversion from self-character to Jesus-character and your battles over this principle are not against flesh and blood, but against powers and principalities in spiritual places. For believers, these battles are in the mind (thoughts) for control over the soul (personality and priorities). Evil has no authority over believers unless the believer entertains evil in his mind. Thoughts contrary to God's will for us are as flaming darts attacking the believer. God provides for us faith (trust) to use as a shield against them being dwelt on in the mind and scripture to fight back against their source as a sharp sword would be used against a physical foe. The battle is in the mind and the outcome is subject to self-will. If self-will chooses to entertain or receive the evil and it penetrates to the heart it becomes sin because it violates the union of the Holy Spirit to the heart or spirit of the believer. If the dart or thought or temptation is rejected to go no further than the mind and is repelled or rejected through not being dwelled on, it was simply a temptation and the battle was won.

One way to think of the spiritual places is to think of a dimension co-existing with our four dimensions of height, width, length, and time some of whose beings can observe us but are barred by God, the Creator of all, from having physical contact with us except in highly limited situations. An analogy is the air around us. If it is calm and clean, we cannot see, feel, or hear it. That doesn't mean it is not there.

Our ability to open and close spiritual doors is initiated with our minds; our thought processes. With our minds we can pray, whether to the one true God whose only begotten Son is Jesus Christ, or to any other god of our choosing. Our thoughts can be in accordance with His directives through the Bible or contrary to them. Our spiritual thoughts directly affect our physical actions and our physical actions directly affect our spiritual health. Our Lord guided us through Paul when he wrote to dwell on good things (Phil 4:8). When your mind dwells on something spiritual it's like presenting that subject matter to the heart or spirit as food to be considered for consumption. As you train your mind to obey the principals of God by submitting those thoughts to the Lord for His evaluation prior to receiving them into your heart for consumption the time spent on the topic becomes longer if it is good and shorter if it's evil. For, your self-will submits more and more to the Lord. As believers, we are subject to different rules of expectations than are non-believers. WE are told by the Bible to put off the old man and put on the new man in the likeness of Christ {Eph 4:22-24). How do we do that?

First, we have to know what the new man should look like by reading the Bible. Then, when we see a character trait of ours which is contrary to His, we focus or purpose to deal with that and change. When the old man sticks up his head you come at him with a biblical truth to block him with your shield and a scripture to proclaim what the new man is to look like with your sword. If possible, verbalize the scripture even if only a whisper to proclaim the manifold wisdom of God to the powers and principalities in heavenly places. Then through your helmet of salvation ask your Father to help you to submit to His Spirit within you to strengthen your new man. Dwell on His word as to how you want to be. Your breastplate of doing things right (righteousness) will thicken, your security of truth will tighten around you as you approach His Kingdom in that specific character trait. Repeat, repeat, repeat, knowing He is at work in your life, making His changes for you one step at a time because you are submitting your self-will to Him to become His reflection. As it begins, it is a suffering experience. But we can have fellowship with Jesus Christ as we suffer. For He, although He was God incarnate, suffered as we in overcoming His human self to be our High Priest (Heb1:14-16).

Our struggle is the putting off the old man of the flesh and putting on the new man provided by the Holy Spirit. He, the Holy Spirit, will not control our Father-given self-will. Otherwise, He would diminish His creation. Our mind has to redirect our self-will, our priorities. We will, undoubtedly, all suffer disappointments or losses, but we can minimize our losses. There is nothing wrong with working to minimizing our losses. We do so my reinforcing our spiritual armor (Ro 13:12-14, Eph 6:11-18) and sharpening our swords with His Word, the Bible. Then USING them. We have to PUT ON the armor and PICK UP the sword. Sitting around whining about what is happening that you don't like is like submitting to your enemy. Love the Lord your God with your STRENGTH! Be transformed into a warrior against evil by renewing you MIND with the Word. You have the Spirit of God joined to your HEART. Let you SOUL change to the character of God. Win!!!!!

Again, we will, undoubtedly, all suffer some disappointments or losses, but we can, through self-will minimize our losses whether they are failures to stand and overcome a temptation or adding wood, hay, and stubble to the foundation of Jesus. We have the God-given right to choose, but we have to claim that right by renewing our mind. Stop thinking about that old carnality of your old self and think of how the new self is to reflect the image of our Lord Jesus Christ. The provision God has made for us when we fail is simply heart felt repentance. Repentance involves asking forgiveness from the Father AND pursuing the reversal of our direction i.e., pressing the putting on of the new man in the image of Christ Jesus; the change of character. As the Church, our charge is to manifest (make obvious) the manifold (multifaceted) wisdom (applied knowledge) of God. So, we are looking for what God would do in a given situation. We have as our example the life of Jesus Christ and the writings of the Apostles, especially the letters to the churches. What we search for is what will reveal the fruit of the Spirit in any given situation that would challenge our ability to do so. Our personal priorities have to change. As previously stated, it is important to realize that one major purpose of the Church is to reveal or manifest to the powers and principalities in heavenly places the manifold wisdom of God (Eph 3:9-12). Realizing and accepting as your personal purpose the pleasing of our living God is to do this, have a character change. That is your purpose if you are part of His Church, the Body and Bride of Christ Jesus. There may well be what appears to be another calling or callings for you, but whatever it may be, it is a subdivision of this one calling of the Church.

What is and how do we manifest God's manifold wisdom? Wisdom is the application of knowledge. God's manifold wisdom is the application of the multifaceted knowledge of God proving His ways triumph over evil. He wants His Church to be triumphant when dealing with evil. He wants to humiliate those evil beings, the fallen angels, before all His creation for challenging His authority before He pronounces His final judgement upon them. (Luke 8:28). He chose the weakness of man to manifest this great truth to His creation. When His manifold or multifaceted wisdom is revealed to His creation by His Church, you and me, those who are followers of the Lamb in the book of The Revelation are encouraged and rejoice before Him. Those who are not His followers are humiliated before Him. For, you see, those who have fallen chose to try to exalt themselves above God their creator. Filled with lies they believed their own lies. They --- are the fallen angels.

Sometime you will find yourself confronted with making a decision to turn to the right or turn to the left. If neither way is sinful and you simply aren't sure what He wants you to do, for He does have a plan for you, pray for God to direct your heart, for your heart is in union with His Spirit. Then wait. Then, perhaps wait some more. When your Heavenly Father directs your heart, His Spirit within you is in control and though a little anxious, you will have peace that even if you are wrong, because you are seeking to please Him, He will guide you through the direction you choose. But listen, for He speaks quietly (1Kings 19:11-13). Read the Proverbs and don't confuse His guidance with emotions. Pray for sound wisdom, judgement, and discretion for applying His word to your life.

Daily we are confronted with situations which challenge our character. So, how are we to deal with them? First, recognize that physical sin has a spiritual root. We cannot see the root of a tree, but without the root the tree cannot stand. So, when you are confronted with making a decision whether or not to physically do something you are thinking about, look for the character trait you will choose to manifest. For example: The act of lying is a physical sin. The words we speak will be directed by self-will whether to reveal a character trait of, perhaps, self-exaltation (exaggerating for personal recognition) or humility. There is a suffering involved in either case. If you don't lie, in this case to exalt yourself in the eyes of the listener, they may not be impressed by your words and not praise you. But, by overcoming that fear and telling the truth you have just won a spiritual battle. The holy angels have been encouraged and the fallen angels have just been shamed before all creation, and there is no guilt for you. At the same time, you have manifested spiritual courage and placed your trust in your Lord that by doing what is right He will support you. Such is an act of trust or faith. Wow, look what such a simple act of faith can do. By the way, if by self-will you had chosen to lie, just the opposite might well have happened. Repentance would have been in order and you could well anticipate the return of the same type of spiritual challenge or temptation and the same struggle to be experienced again. It will not be any easier the next time unless you chose to trust the Lord this time. Temptations become less and less a challenge as your character changes to reflect that of Christ, i.e., as the new man replaces the old. Believers are under a different set of rules than non-believers.

Many years ago, I was complaining to a very good friend about what a bad day I just had. Repeatedly, I expressed dissatisfaction about my day. I guess my friend let me dig a big hole for myself. Finally, he looked at me and asked, "Well, did you ask the Lord to place your day in order?" Being unwilling at that point to tell him the truth, I replied "Yes". "Well then, what are you griping about?", was his final reply and the conversation ended. That principle of asking the Lord to order my day stuck with me, not to mention the "privilege" of going around the mountain again to be confronted with similar situations I could win or lose along with opportunities to tell embarrassing truths. I really don't remember if I ever repented to him for not being truthful in that situation. It would have been good for me to have done so. It would have been encouraging to him for me to have done so, also. I did repent to God, and He has granted me that memory for my encouragement. My dear friend has gone on to be with the Lord now. I believe he has a fire-proof jewel for his question and statement to me.

I want to help you take the Bible out of the abstract and into practical application. Usually, when presented with something we don't like, we are in fact faced with a spiritual confrontation. Is our reaction going to manifest deeds of the flesh or the fruit of the Spirit? If you are not sure what the fruit of the Spirit refers to, look it up and put it to memory so you will know how to act (Gal 5:22-23). What happens to us is not nearly as important as how we react to what happens to us. The situation and how we react to it frequently occur with a split second separating the two. So, preparation prior to conflict is very important. If our military did not train for combat and our country was attacked, we would be in sad shape. Our personal spiritual training comes from reading the Bible and understanding what was just read. I'm not knocking Bible scholars or anyone who wants to study the original Greek or Hebrew writings, but such is not reasonable for most of us. I suggest you download Webster's dictionary or something similar and a bible app on your phone. I have the YouVersion which gives me many different translations to compare. By looking up definitions and by comparing different translations, I can usually feel confident about the truth being presented by the scripture. The most surprising thing I have found is how many words I think I know the definition of but actually don't. If I cannot confidently define a word in a verse, I look up its definition. It only takes a few seconds and to misunderstand the meaning of just one word will distort the entire verse. We are talking about a portion of your sword and shield!!

We are creatures of habit. Develop a habit of reading and understand just one verse per day if you are not reading the Bible often. And if you miss a day, just start back up when you remember and ask the Lord to help you to remember to do more. As you understand what you are reading, the Holy Spirit within you will awaken your desire to learn more. If you start out too fast, your flesh will cry out too loudly and you will not continue for many days. If you miss a day, don't be surprised and allow condemnation to set in. Rejoice before the Lord that He is providing a way for you to sharpen your sword and thicken your shield. Read a verse, any verse. Combat condemnation with thanksgiving to the Lord. You just won a battle. Don't complicate things. Remember there is a simplicity and purity of devotion to Christ.

Mentally or verbally quoting a scripture forces the mind to focus on the good things of God when facing a challenge to our faith. Grouping scriptures together in a form of prayer, as long as the contextual meaning of the different verses is not affected, is great. We are talking about transforming the MIND to LOVE (obey without being burdened to do so) God. My most used phrases throughout my days personally are: He will never leave me nor forsake me ....Behold, I am with you always...........
Help me Father.........That I might know Him and the power of His resurrection, the fellowship of His sufferings, being conformed to His death that I might attain to the resurrection from the dead and manifest the manifold wisdom of God to the powers and principalities in high places, that being Christ in me, the hope of glory (You would be surprised how fast that group of scriptures can be thought)...........Blessed be

the name of the Lord our God who delivers us from our enemies……..
Father, I pray that You would place this day in order…………Help me
Lord to be pleasing to You this day………..Be sovereign Lord and help
me to walk through this. There are others that come to mind in different
situations, but this gives you the idea. Again, what happens to us is not
so important as how we react to what happens to us. It's a little hard to
pray a prayer of submission without asking for the good things we would
really like to happen, and I certainly do pray for specifics at times, but we
walk into the unknown every day. I find overcoming the old-self exciting.
Challenges occur and faith (trust) has to take over. By the way, only we
and God know our thoughts and our motives. No place in the Bible does
it suggest differently. Don't let the master of lies and trickery make you
think otherwise. Vain reasonings and speculations will hit your shield a
lot. As your sword sharpens your shield of trust thickens.

If you have trouble memorizing scripture, you might try this technique.
The English language is written in sentences but read in phrases. The
English language / is written / in sentences / but read / in phrases. Do you
see what I mean? Take the first phrase of a sentence and repeat it several
times until it becomes boring. Then add the second phrase and repeat the
combination until it becomes boring. Then add the next phrase and repeat
the whole thing until it becomes boring, and so on and so on until the
entire sentence is boring to repeat. You have just put it to memory. Then
add the first phrase of the next sentence. Repeat the first sentence with the
first phrase of the second until it becomes boring. That joins the second
sentence to the end of the first. Add a phrase and repeat, add a phrase and
repeat, add a phrase and repeat. It's slow, but it works. Train your mind
via your God given self-will to do it. Be ye therefor transformed by the
renewing of your mind. Bring every thought captive to obedience to His
word. Put on the new man. Be a faithful worker rightly dividing the word
of truth. Sharpen that sword!!

Heb: 5:8 "He learned obedience through His sufferings." Think of this
scripture. Jesus learned something. This scripture cannot be referring to
His crucifixion because sufferings is plural and He learned obedience from
them. He was never disobedient because that would have been sin so the
sufferings were not punishments. As were the sufferings of Jesus referred
to in this scripture, our sufferings occur during the transition from the old

man to the new. Although Jesus was God-incarnate He was also man and because He was man He was able to be tempted. James 1:13 states that God cannot be tempted nor does He tempt anyone. But Hebrews says Jesus was tempted in all things just as we are, only without sin. Only the man-Jesus could be tempted and His sufferings was the process of transition from His human fleshly character which could be tempted to sin, although He never entered into sin, to Godly character which was dead to the temptation of sin. That process caused Him suffering just as it causes us suffering. Him being God incarnate enabled Him to overcome his flesh and the Holy Spirit within us enables us to overcome our flesh, only because that is what the Father wants to happen.

The old character doesn't "die" peacefully. Peace, from the Prince of Peace, reigns as the new man has replaced the old. Jesus experienced His sufferings of transition without ever falling into sin. And, as with Jesus the man, the spiritual battle is for the soul of man. Our personalities are ours as individuals. But when the Father looks upon our souls, He wants them all to look as reflections of Jesus the Christ. As stated before, our souls are what distinguish us as individuals, one from another. Our Father wants all of our souls to reflect the character of His Son. Why? For His glory before all He has created, exemplifying the church manifesting the manifold wisdom of God by applying His Word to defeat evil. What an amazing privilege He has granted His children.

Read the following while thinking about the principle explained in the previous paragraph.

Take these three scriptures: (NAS)

Phil 3:7-14 But whatever things were gain to me, those things I have counted as loss for the sake of Christ. More than that, I count all things to be loss in view of the surpassing value of knowing Christ Jesus my Lord, for whom I have suffered the loss of all things, and count them but rubbish so that I may gain Christ, and may be found in Him, not having a righteousness of my own derived from the Law, but that which is through faith in Christ, the righteousness which comes from God on the basis of faith, that I may know Him and the power of His resurrection and the fellowship of His sufferings, being transformed to His death; in order that I may attain to the resurrection from the dead. Not that I have already obtained it or have already become perfect, but I press on so that I may lay hold of that for which also I was laid hold of by Christ Jesus. Brethren, I do not regard myself as having laid hold of it yet; but one thing I do: forgetting what lies behind and reaching forward to what lies ahead, I press on toward the goal for the prize of the upward call of God in Christ Jesus.

Eph 3:8-12 To me, the very least of all saints, this grace was given, to preach to the Gentiles the unfathomable riches of Christ, and to bring to light what is the administration of the mystery which for ages has been hidden in God who created all things; so that the manifold wisdom of God might now be made known through the church to the rulers and the authorities in the heavenly places. This was in accordance with the eternal purpose which He carried out in Christ Jesus our Lord, in whom we have boldness and confident access through faith in Him.

Col 1:25-27 Of this church I was made a minister according to the stewardship from God bestowed on me for your benefit, so that I might fully carry out the preaching of the word of God, that is, the mystery which has been hidden from the past ages and generations, but has now been manifested to His saints, to whom God willed to make known what is the riches of the glory of this mystery among the Gentiles, which is Christ in you, the hope of glory.

The key to understanding the Phil. Scripture is understanding that it is not referring to His death on the cross or His eternal resurrection from being dead. Those events validated the truth of this scripture, but this scripture is not referring to them. "That I might know Him" Paul was miraculously called to be an apostle. He had been prepared by God all his life to be able to function in the Church as a gift to the Church, certainly for us gentiles. But after his ministry was well established and functioning, he writes "That I might know Him". To know Him here is referring to a one-ness with Christ in every spiritual way, fulfilling what is referred to in Eph 5-30-32 likening Christ and the Church to the marriage of a man and a woman. "And the power of His resurrection" here refers to Jesus' human self-will being totally submitted to the Father and Him finding the life in pleasing the Father in every situation with temptation no longer causing suffering because there was no self-centeredness left. This was a process which occurred throughout His life [just as it is a process which will occur throughout our lives], the last bit dying at the garden in prayer. Paul was wanting to experience and live in the full expression of Jesus Christ through man, i.e., the power of spiritual victory in every situation. When Jesus won His final warfare with fleshly self-will in the garden before His arrest, He knew what was about to happen. Every instinct of protecting His body and resisting the pain to come was crying out – screaming if you will – to protect self. He knew the false accusations and public humiliations were coming. He knew He would be beaten and tortured cruelly and mercilessly. He knew the nails would be driven through His hands and feet and He would hang for hours on that cross. He knew breathing would be a struggle and painful as He pressed against the nails to raise His body with outstretched arms and crossed feet to allow air to enter His lungs and that the relief of death, though inevitable, would not come quickly. He could avoid it all by rejecting His Father's will and walking away – obeying his flesh. His flesh's final resistance was overcome as He focused His mind to reject it and to submit His body for the sacrifice sufficient for all mankind to be presented clean before the Father. The sacrificial Lamb of God was ready to reach 'It is finished' (Jn 19:30). His resurrection from dying to His fleshly self-will 'If possible, take this cup from Me' was attained (obtained with effort) by His decision "non-the-less, Thy will be done". His completed spiritual "resurrection" had occurred giving Him strength to walk out His last day of this life. Hallelujah, hallelujah, hallelujah, amen!

The word 'faith' can be rather abstract. My hope in this writing is to take the abstract of some scripture and help you to see the practicality of its application. Faith can simply be defined as trust; and works can simply be defined as behavior. If you believe Jesus Christ is the Son of God and that the only way to the Father is through Him, that belief is only proven real by praying to Him a repentance prayer requesting salvation. Once done, the Holy Spirit takes residence within you with your body becoming His tabernacle or dwelling place and joins to your spirit as the earnest or guarantee of your salvation. He does not want you to sin or be destructive to His tabernacle (1 Cor 6:19, 3:11-17) Recognition – prayer—trust – behavior – Life is simple. There is as simplicity and purity of devotion to Christ (2 Cor 1:12, 11:13) that is so easily distorted by our adversaries and made complex by well-meaning brothers and sisters. Don't hunt for a law that you can live by to make yourself acceptable to God.

The question I raise to you now is not that of your eternal salvation, but rather how can you win the daily warfare you as a Christian will most assuredly face on a frequent if not daily basis. First, you will lose grand opportunities to be pleasing to your heavenly Father if you do not read the Bible. The word of God is your sword for offensive battle while faith or trust is your defensive shield. When the Lord Jesus was taken after fasting and shown by Satan all He could have by worshiping him, the devil, Jesus' reply was not a great oration against the devil, but simply the Word of God. Focus on the new -testament and proverbs. In the new-testament, the Book of John and the letters to the different churches provide a sharp sword, though not a completed work without the rest. When confronted with a physical challenge, recognize there is a spiritual challenge associated with it. To win the spiritual challenge is pleasing to God the Father because you have sought first His Kingdom and His righteousness (Ro 14:17-19) and righteousness is simply doing things right. Jesus promised the Father knows our physical needs before we do and will provide for us what we need if we FIRST seek His sovereignty in willful submission and seek doing what is right in His eyes.

You next need to memorize some scripture for your sword. God loves His Word in the form of Jesus and in the form of the Bible. He honors His Word when humbly presented to Him. When Jesus was asked how to pray by one of His disciples (Matt 6:9-13) He replied with what we know as the Lord's Prayer. He said first to acknowledge to the Father that we understand who He, the Father, is and that He is holy. Then, ask Him for what you should be seeking, that His sovereignty would be revealed and His will would reign in this situation. Then ask for the 'bread' you want along with the strength to forgive others the way you want Him to forgive you. I have always found it interesting the importance God has on us having a forgiving heart. It is linked to peace, our peace. I am sure there are many books written and sermons preached of forgiving those who have hurt us unjustly. If we do something which gives someone the right to cause us pain then this scripture is really not very applicable, but when someone hurts us without "justification" we are instructed to forgive them. That is a tough one. And, I can speak from experience that holding on to the resentment of being unjustly treated is devastating spiritually. Resentment does not die on its own. You can suppress it for a time, perhaps for years, but it will not die without you spiritually killing it and as it grows into more and more severe resentment it can change to hate.

The book of 1ˢᵗ John teaches that to hate a brother in Christ is to be guilty of murder and murder is a character trait of the devil (Jn 8:44). I urge you to deal with resentment before it becomes hate. In my past I harbored resentment and the Father chastised me by withholding His peace more and more as my resentment grew and grew. Finally, I looked up the definition of hate and realized I was all but there. Just as resentment can evolve into hate so can chastisement evolve into judgement. My fear of His judgement far outweighed the satisfaction in the flesh of hate. I prayed for Him to show me how to escape the pain and He showed me the simplicity of the path I was to take. After I was obedient with humility and truth, He blessed me with a freedom I had not felt in a very long time. He will do the same for you if you find yourself in the trap of resentment. He is no respecter of persons. We can all come to Him with our burdens. He will give us the strength to obey His word. He will break those chains which would bind us into uselessness.

There are no magic words we can present to God to get Him to do our will. He is who He is and we are who we are and that will never change. He wants us to recognize His sovereignty. That is an example of His manifold or multifaceted wisdom. We are privileged to understand that. The Lord's Prayer is a reminder to us of that and His system of priorities. He wants us to be a forgiving people who recognize His loving kindness to forgive us. Present His Word to Him to remind yourself actually more than to remind Him of His promises. Trust Him in prayer to fulfill His Word.

There is an important principle we, as Christians, very easily overlook because we are the recipients of the graciousness of God and focus so much on His loving kindness and forgiveness. That principle is revealed in the book of Luke in the parable of the prodigal son. Jesus taught here for the encouragement of believers how our heavenly Father welcomes our return to Him if we, for a time, fall away. The prodigal son took his inheritance prematurely and squandered all of it on fleshly indulgences. Then the unexpected situations in which he found himself led him to want to return home if even as a servant. When he did return home, his father welcomed him with great joy and received him honorably back into his house. Then the faithful older son complained, feeling slighted. His father's reply was the necessity of receiving back his younger son whom he thought he had lost; and then he said to the older son "all that I have is yours". In other words, the younger son had already received his inheritance and all the father then possessed belonged to his older son who had been faithful. Perhaps some of what the father would acquire later on would go to the younger son, but there were consequences for the younger son's actions. For the believer, there are consequences for deliberate acts of rebellion against the ways of God. Consequences that the Lord will help the believer walk through, but forgiveness of the sin does not wipe out the physical consequences of that sin. Again, the Lord will forgive the sin of the believer who repents, but there may well be things set in motion while the sin was active in the believer's life which the forgiven believer may have to walk through. Such is a very good reason to reject that sinful temptation in the first place.

Next, as I have stated before, understand that you, as part of the Church, are to reveal by your actions the manifold wisdom of God to the powers and principalities in heavenly places. That is His calling for your goal in this life on this earth as ordained by God (Eph 3:12). And, when you do so, not only will you win that spiritual battle you have been confronted with, but you will have pleased your heavenly Father, encouraged the holy angels, some of which He may well send to help you, and openly humiliate the fallen angels who rebelled against the one true God.

Jesus won every challenge every time. The character of Jesus in you will win every challenge every time. When you manifest the fruit of the Holy Spirit instead of the deeds of the flesh, you win every time. As believers our priorities are different than they used to be. Winning the spiritual should become paramount in our lives once we realize its importance to the Father. When our priorities line up with His, He is faithful to take care of our earthly needs for He is pleased by our physical behavior demonstrating the spiritual values which motivate them. Vain reasons and speculations are blocked by our shield and the pathway we follow is opened by our sword as the Holy Spirit guides.

Every spiritual confrontation eventually challenges the peace within us. Pay attention to what is happening to you on a spiritual basis. Use the Word to strike down what conflicts with it. Remember, what happens to you is not nearly as important as how you react to what happens to you. If you find yourself in a pit, over and over and over again, perhaps you should stop clawing at the loose ground around you. Pray for a ladder. Then, when the ladder He provides you looks too short, take the first step and see what happens.

God did not save us to be wishi-washi, helpless baby Christians ruled by our flesh and waiting for death so we can go to Heaven. I'm not belittling Heaven in the least. But, how does that behavior reveal His manifold wisdom to anyone now? Stand up and be counted as one willing to put on Christ so you can reveal the Kingdom of God to all creation by your behavior. Be a man of integrity or a woman of virtue able to rightly divide the Word of truth and capable of demonstrating the power of His resurrection. Grow spiritually and seek His sovereignty revealed through you by your daily behavior.

I know personally when I began praying for His daily sovereignty in my life, I was a bit nervous. What kind of challenge was I opening myself up for? What bad thing was going to happen to show me my weakness and drive me to repentance? Was I being arrogant before the Lord? Well, first thing, the Lord does not tempt us and He is fully capable and willing to limit the situations which arise to what we are spiritually strong enough to overcome by applying the Word we know. God is not sadistic. We are to enter the day with spiritual humility before Him and the honest desire to experience more deeply His Kingdom of righteousness, peace, and joy in the Holy Spirit. We can please Him by relying on Him to help us by showing us how to apply His Word and reveal His ways by our behavior. He has promised if our ways, not our words, if our ways acknowledge Him, He will make our paths straight (Prov 3:5-7).

As we draw to a close:

Seek first the Kingdom of God and His righteousness …. Luke 12:29-32

Our battle is not against flesh and blood, but against spiritual authorities in the heavenly places …Eph 6:12

Put on the full armor of God …. Eph 6:11-18

Put off the old man and put on the new man in the image of Christ ….Eph 4:22

Fulfill the purpose of the Church …. Eph 3:9-12

What about joy, peace and happiness?

"I came that they may have life, and have it abundantly." (Jn 10:10) Prior to believing, we were "dead in our trespasses and sins." (Eph 2:1, Ro 6) Jesus gives us life when we are born again by His Holy Spirit upon salvation. The life more abundantly comes as we convert from our old ways (referred to as the flesh) to our new ways which are His ways which are spiritual. Because the Father has set spiritual laws which affect the physical and because He wants us to reveal His wisdom to all creation, He has established a cause/effect system which He has chosen to be fact. He will not change it for you or for me. Our priorities have to change. Spiritually, we are to be transformed into the image of Christ. This is not a pretend thing, pretending that when the Father looks at us, He sees Jesus Christ. No, no, no. When the Father looks at us, He sees us as we really are, but overlooks our immaturities so long as our sights are on pleasing Him. He rejoices only when we exemplify the character of Jesus Christ. To accomplish this our decision-making-processes have to change from focus on self to focus on the Father. Our focus on the Father is only granted through Jesus our Savior being allowed by our self-will to be Jesus our Lord; and our submission to the guidance of the Holy Spirit who dwells within God's established temples – you and me. Our trust via self-will must be in Him, God the Holy Spirit, to help us to set aside the old man's character of fleshly self, i.e., selfishness, greed, envy, strife, idolatry, adultery, theft, lying, cheating, laziness, undependability, drunkenness, and all the other many "me's" of this flesh and put on Jesus's character of love, joy, peace, gentleness, goodness, faith, meekness, temperance, etc., the fruit of the Spirit. Trust me, you cannot succeed to change absent resentment or hypocrisy without the Helper – the Holy Spirit changing your heart (spirit) first to match His and He will not do that without your submission to the Father by way of Jesus Christ the Son. Actions that appear to be change if accomplished by self, will be short-lived. We must constantly depend upon the Lord to give us the strength to please Him. Love the Lord your God with all your strength.

First things first: "Seek first the Kingdom of God, and His righteousness". Seek means to pursue, chase, eagerly want to find. Kingdom means area of sovereign reign or control. Righteousness simply means doing things right. His righteousness means doing things right – God's way. So, if we eagerly pursue God's sovereignty in our lives through our willful submission to Him and yield to doing things His way with His help, in His timing, He promises to provide for our physical needs and more since He knows them before we even ask and that is what He wants to do. "I have never seen the righteous forsaken, nor his seed begging bread." (Ps 37:25) To be strong in the Lord is to spiritually hold tightly to His principles or ways. To understand the ways of God is much more important than observing His acts or actions in the short term. Understanding the ways of God is to understand, as much as He allows, why He does what He does. A good question to ask yourself is "Why do I do what I do?".

Love the Lord your God with all your heart, mind, soul, and strength. One character trait at a time, be obedient to His Word without it being burdensome to you with all your spirit which has been joined to His, with all your thoughts and reasonings, with all your personality and individuality, and with all your determination and focus. Put off the old man and put on the new in the image of Christ our Lord by the renewing of your mind. Trust in the Lord with all your heart, lean not on your own understanding. In all your WAYS acknowledge Him and He will make your path straight.

The battles we face are in our minds. The fiery darts of fear and doubt are commonly in the form of speculations and vain reasonings about the future concerning any particular issue. Condemnation about our past, regrets about what we did or did not do, questioning our own value, and so forth and so on. The list is endless concerning the topics of the darts. But how they are presented are all lies, from the father of lies. Our defense is the shield of faith or trust and it gets thicker and stronger as we consume the written Word of God while simultaneously our sword of the Spirit gets stronger and sharper. As we pursue His righteousness our breastplate for defense gets stronger and we can walk in peace. We are tightly secured in truth, and, of course, we have no access to any of these without first having the helmet of salvation.

As you win the battles and accomplish your calling, the satisfaction of knowing you have demonstrated by your behavior the manifold wisdom of God, will grant you an unspeakable joy. Happiness will follow suit as you demonstrate by your life that your God truly is the Lord; and you will find peace in your life because you can forget what lies behind and press on to your own upward calling of God.

I urge you. Fulfill your purpose by pressing on to accomplish what only you can do. Dscover for yourself "Happy is the people whose God is the Lord" (Ps 144:15).

I hope what I have shared with you is of help to you throughout this life. Perhaps, when we are on our knees before Him someday, we will meet one another.

The following are a couple of poems I hope you enjoy.

Addendum

Enough

Enough! Enough! Our debts are paid!
His blood Christ poured before God's throne.
Accept His grace by trust alone.
Your sins forgiven
My sins forgiven
Exchanged for robes cleansed purest white,
That blood-stained cross turned tree of life.

'Twas His choice before all time
To set this stage called life of mine,
To let me choose, self-will He gave
To turn to Him to stop the pain
of loneliness – uncertain times.
The fear of life, much less what lies
Behind the curtain blocking sight
Past my last breath, when heartbeat stops.
Blessed be-yond concept of mind

To live beyond the endless time.
Because of Him and Him alone
My heart shall dwell before His throne.
My breath be given by His grace.
His presence granting me a place to

Worship Him beyond all time
To see His glory close, and mine;
Reflection only of His own.

I cannot stand, myself alone.
I am undone and prostrate fall
Before His presence for all time,
And yet without a change of time
Be lifted up to stand before – perhaps beside.
How shall I be, and why?
Except to please Him and thereby
To serve His will and take my place as He prescribes.

Rejoice! Rejoice! My debts are paid!
The Father drew me to the Son,
I saw the truth, I was undone
And helpless could not go beyond
That point without His touch.
I was not denied, and still my spirit
Soars because of Him!
My life now His, yet oh how I rejoice
His life is mine.
That bloodstained cross
For me turned tree of life.

How precious did the Father draw
My searching soul to His dear Son.
He made the way,
He paid the price of loneliness
In life as man.
No blemish found, no stain within or out.

I could have been as He,
But chose my way not His throughout my life.
With no excuse to justify myself
Before God's throne and purity of light.

In darkness to abide except His blood acknowledged
And accepted in this life.
One way alone was made for me.
Christ paid that price
And changed from red to white
My robe as seen by all in future time.
That bloodstained cross,
For me turned tree of life.

Purpose

In Jesus' name I pray today
His power through me be on display,
Discourag-ing those who betrayed.
Exalting self they sought to rise
Above the Maker - of the skies
And all creation – even them.
The everlasting wrong, they chose
To war against the Lord of hosts.
Their sentence waiting 'til that time
The Father says "Enough!
Ven-geance is Mine!"
The bles-sed Lamb seen as 'twas slain
His whole creation views the Same
And all He is shall be revealed.
His judgement true, He shall not yield.
In Jesus' name I pray today
His power through me be on display,
His holy angels smile when I
Prefer His way o'r that of mine,
And die a little bit to self.
Preferring Him and life He gives,
Through me a bit of Him revealed.
All hail the pow'r of Jesus' name!
All hail! His glory shall remain.
His mys-ter-y through me revealed
'though through the ages was concealed.
Salvation more than Heaven be
It's Christ my Lord revealed in me.
In Jesus' name I'm blessed to pray
His pow'r be seen through me this day,
His wisdom hidden through the a-ges
Now I see
'Tis Christ in me.

Printed in the United States
by Baker & Taylor Publisher Services